A HAUNTING WITHOUT

Joshua Jones is a writer from the UK who currently lives in San Francisco. Their most recent publication is *Diametric Fist Tender* (Pilot Press, 2020), a poem from which was anthologized in *100 Queer Poems* (Penguin, 2022).

Also by Joshua Jones

Diametric Fist Tender   (Pilot Press, 2020)

CONTENTS

ISBN: 978-1-916938-37-3

Cover designed by Aaron Kent

Cover art: © Fran_kie / Adobe Stock

Typeset by Aaron Kent

Broken Sleep Books Ltd
PO BOX 102
Llandysul
SA44 9BG

A Haunting Without Allegory

Joshua Jones

Broken Sleep Books

RED DOOR

for Sean Bonney

shadows filled the streets. & up above

How flesh in restless sleep restrained from knowing
Or all too buoyant stretched upon the impasse
Rocks in medias res on wine-dark seas
Named for privacy & its upholding
Against the fire without that threatens rage
More palpably in daylight sprung from murk
Should it better chance to see, yet fearful
Of iris charred by ghosts left unallayed

1.

In skin under sun batons
Fall like night across your face.

It's spicy on the streets this evening
Pulled into a car they say who

Are you, dissembled into flesh unmade
By siren song & bullet pocks

Upon the shell of what is named
When cops speak — the sound

Of glass irrupting, its laughter track
Of burning in reverse, as choppers shred

Night to sheets that settle on the lake
& melt as dawn interpellates the shadows,

Now fucking answer.

2.

eradicate me says the dream
of moral rectitude

        on street feast

        & euphemized flesh, smoke

thickening the mission in a fog
of unattributed

            i find my voice you

            not washed

            into the guttered sea, we are that

cackle splashing back, perturbed
an image of collapse upon
perpetually embroaching shore, the fear retracts
like glass thru sand & soft

            focus bronze

alighting from the ocean & the sun
our haptic chalkline grasp
at oar

3.

To hear your speeches on another shore
I see myself as what's yet unbecome.

Water is scary. The ocean in complete disdain
For agency extends. Mélange

Of bodies, how its rising corpse
Gets born again on surface, stands then sinks

Back down in debt. You enter into them
Like the world, without consent, abrupt

Against the other enthorned fingers
Stealing continuity from the store

To carve on wood the work of living
Sunlight cannot read, its mouth in forest

Forming from a cob heart ghosts
To smear in facets of refuse.

4.

this landlord's hands

this man he wants to become

in the sink, salt & blood, in the eyes

of a low world scattered off

in glass & light & locked doors

they are eating under the surface his legs

in the swamp his language unobstructed

gruel his story softens like rain

across the streets into something contained

like dog vomit, sideway flash of fox & fetid pity, i warm

to him thru sleep in the destitution of better judgment,

the violence of a fist around your own pathetic throat

5.

Thru porch ribs life
Painted on the living
Scene choked out to face

Staring back from pillow
No vacancy, all the harm
You have done when no

One is looking back they
Did it all they did nothing
Left when who is not looking

Back. No handle
No way all the dogs of the world
Tails tucked to soil coughed

Sud of being right of being
Wrong in tacked mirror slack
Lung a perforated sheet

A broken heart no insipid
Skin tucked into keyboard
Flocked the people lost no heart

Burn across the scorched rib
Cage to do not living to do not
Hurt another day, & take the body

Out into the clouds & see it weather
Slit of wrinkle slit of river slit of
Never going back there from again

6.

Where the shoreline meets the forest meets the rent
Burden, about sleep the landlords are getting unruly
At the mouth here I'll place this mask for you gently

Your body like a land mass leaving the world behind
For whatever that ocean & all its flames might want to say
To you as gulping down the violence you chose. Our

Salary wrapped in plastic around your death, ventilated
In the brutal morning of grass climbing its slight persistent grasp
Around the pillar once they called a spine, an economy

Of coughs trickling down, like piss, like a lover dying again
In your tired arms, that you sent into the murky checks & balances
Of guttural sky, that open bruise, that premonition of a better ghost

To come & haunt you. This is how it looks to watch your family
Die, that they had no choice, that your living tongue moves
In them, as they tend the lawn & reluctant lungs abate

The noise of what it felt like just to be you. We pin that badge
Of your silken face in freezer, slick upon thaw, a stray dog
Chasing down the warmth at the end of fear, at the end

Of the sentence curdling down your chin, the pool of flames
At your feet polished our back into fresher air, the flicked skin
Skimming like blustered cloud on blue from night collapsed.

7.

An angel is the monster
On horizon tips a warning
That your spirit like a dizzy grounded bird

Barely makes, a cage on porch
On mouth they've spelled initials
Spelling doom, & on the water

Carcass light, the sound of every color
Turned to screaming turned to home
As hope held a monster raised that

Angel never was & never will be
Sheds its gender into air & hopeful
Foam against the crumpling city walls, it pleads

Against a pane of fading glass & green
Wrapped like film around its body wanting
But to breathe a single glimmer spun

From what you said a sun could plead
To mean from in its cage, a single letter
Dropped into the stream that filters out

& soil eats, that grass could with a single prayer
Denounce, & put to dreaming, put that language
Back to better crux, from which

A body barely & composed emerges, holds the gaze
Of scary welcome light from its new eyes
& answers thickly bifurcated want

8.

Your face in noise that hope had slack
& wanting to put shape to wings & bromide
Ever ripples, leash thru dark

& looming green the wooden gate
To mark by, every limit of bone
A body says it will & can't abide. Yes

Get fucked the angels in the end
May not desert you, but their tender
Comes not in form of care but meaning

Left to slither, & when sand
Down every crevice falls the sun won't love you, won't
Be able in its language yet to see

How you in this contingent blink
Had suffered, had held the promise of a name
You couldn't digest, & in it unaffinity

Cried wolf. The forest thus & only lets you enter, calligraphic
Mulch your name had tried to shine & how
This stomach dusk-lit swallows all you uttered

9.

The house has light in spine & sheds
Begrudging, money thru the sky
To open throat. It eats like angels

Paid on cusp, they do not care
Get in they say we're going for
A wellness drive, no weak ones welcome

Here, leave to remain
On melting porch. They have no skin, the only face
Is ocean melting, as the sun

Refutes real distance. It is a choice
Of what you want, to remain distinct
Or become the life within. The life within

Is where light dies in shrugged skin
& upholstery. A bookcase like a forest
Looms like angels over dinner. The angels

Say you'd better finish quick or you will starve.
Your body does not need the food it just thinks
That it wants it. Your body melts like light on sea

& says I thank you angels. The angels pick up
What is left & laugh at why they bothered.

10.

There is a purity in fire of nazi flesh & cop skin
Crackling. It is the sound that angels make
On their best behavior. On the white face

Of your precinct I see myself distorted. I want
It to say fuck the police but the taser
Still trembles. To take the police out of yourself

Stomp the syntax down you breathe by, burn
On the pristine steps of intuition your fucking home
& stand in the flames, like statuary & padlocks

Come undone, the language of a civic hall
Latched into your bones unlearns its words
In fiery song & open mouth with poisoned root

Burning like a mirror fell to glass & charred robe
You hid behind your right to be alive, say no
More, my face is taken, I see it smarting

In the lash of real air, as structures wait
To become smoke & future ghosts, whose fluid light
Might cut into the night fuck the police.

LIGHTHOUSE FIELD

Every petty angel of your best intent is falling
On fire to stack this pillar of incinerated boyfriends.
It stands there like a really big tree. The ashes
Coat the cops as sluggish cumshots. On West
Cliff the wild tongues that sing in the dry but still
Green grass, where your desire became a ghost,
Undusted in rubble & haunted by the future, loam
& hope. There are only two genders. One is a dog
Barking with taut lungs through a hole in the fence
& though you can see it, it sees a void sparking
With mineral light like burnt film decibels
Rising to fall with the pace of its chest. The other
A sieve of pickets & thickening glass, sunlight flung
Through garish chant, followed by wide silence & the sense
Of something yet to come. Today I am both. You said
That knowledge is an impossible object, formed
Not in exchange but in the gap between having
& giving. I said something about whether or not
I could fuck it. In the end it swallowed me whole,
& you too, & our cells merged into somewhere else,
Decanting like fireworks in a dark space, a glottal stomp
Parting us to return, until at its loudest we fall apart
Into bright light, the scene returning to pasty NorCal
March afternoon & a dog that would like us to leave.

ON ACCURACY

Isn't it the law that no fuck off, I thread
My gender thru a horseshoe to stomp
Your face. The point is to make the point

Sharp enough to cut, to sculpt a future
More liveable, to this extent love is a weapon
Carved on ambivalence, soaking up poison

& cure. The point is also to miss
The point, we are not weapon but flesh
We are circumscribed & sore, we have cried

We're alive. The aspiration of breathing to drape
Its wreckage across the wound, to see
The wound as not your own but the wreckage

Precisely. Some days it is enough to walk
Down the street to the sea without drowning
The waves out slowly encroach

Horizon insufflated by falling, I meet
Lovers, continents & islands. It's not
That I don't love you endlessly, rattled

On the carapace, giddily small, but the effort
So much simply to not be undone, the zip
Of our life, shall we meet for breakfast?

KING CURTIS

In the shop the sweets spill on the floor
you have cried a thousand times, imagining life
made out with, lonely blimp of my heart
be bashful in the glare of sweeping lights
on the street where feeding failed. They all want
to eat the sweets, in the centrefold of the city
staring back with basic infinite love
display cramming its mouth down the middle
to never be entered. You cannot have my bacon
you will die but that's why I need it, the songs
are repeatable life & that can't anymore portray
satisfaction. Withdrawal of love is the death of you
I pray for in sincerity every day, just to eat
in the comfort of being a person, chasing
you down, every single sweet that stands its ground to bask
enlightened in the certainty of being scooped back up.

TORQUE

Not a compass nub subdermal
That points without a world but
My love, the sound of breaking

In public, the mirror, the discomfort
Of old friends, a brief directed respite
Pinching dreamlessly. To change

Is endless, the centre melts beneath
But also inside, it is blaring
With history when the simplest gestures

Take hold. For a body to be all that it is
Not yet or was, but impact and bloom
In the swift pass, that's the trail

Of your feet that's the taste of a thirst

PUBLIC POEM OF PRIVATE LOSS

1.

    The old light moves
    Off new air & rain

Falls. It is to unmade worlds we are committed
In the hung & fast space of current happenings.

As salt the knives go, in tundras a semblance
Of maybe, all little delights & the blast of night

Electric unwoven.
                Moving
In all directions
From the catastrophe of shock
To the slow tragedy of remaining, a hand thru the dark
In sleep that jolts.
              There is nothing more literal than a ghost you want
To feel but cannot find. To ask in the sunk gaze
Of nearby sound a question to no one who can.
Awaken for a shift that doesn't exist, a creak
On childhood stair, how the monsters all fade
Into morning itself, the coal of its slit to lung.

2.

And you were in life looking
Not for death but the stillness
Of its future as a promise
To help you sleep.

               Desire

In ricochets from ghosts at step,
The deep untouchable creak of their lilt
No clouds could cover
The gap & its personal monsters
There as your smile folds. I see you
Through ghosts, always, you see
Me too.

        And looking in sleep for a promise
Of the present as something borne
The stillness of an absence passed
On.

3.

    & there is you

In the shifting character of your grief – at length

The flatness of unpunctured grey thru nominal days;

An unexpected pleasant rain to hide your face

In the memory of streets; the blank snow of another's gaze

Lit at look & fading; on diaphragmatic fire heave

The ground as flesh, the coast a gash

On what could not have been, a dipping pulse

At sea to far gone ships; convulsions, ligaments

Unspun, in dawn the light deferred to hear

The privacy of loss, its public speech

A city swept up & out to what comes crashing down,

In lungs on bed, the night now cold & laid

Off, a morning ember

Stubbed or crackling

                    – & me

In the grief of my shifting character

Settled as if in truth on a need to hold

More than its ravels, receding into something

At home against the wave-lit coastal roads

Led out of town & into nights

Of wildfire blackened stubs

On dying, half-lit green.

4.

While the world of things, their insufficiency,
Decries the dead as absent, and holding on

To stillness, as if here, as if contained, belies
Their definite article, the stretching tense

Of limb in heave of torso, the ghost
In a smile continued, when out of nowhere they raise

Their heads as it passes to the sun. They see
You shed, they are your shedding, the days

Stay named, which is the name of how they shake
And nothing makes you less or more

Alone than love's purest cut, given over
To belief in what can mean.

                                    It's not your lost presence swallowed
Into my shape, but I as ghost tracing
In the gaps of your absence, & how
It lasts.

5.

& today life feels good. You would
Have loved it. I ride the wave
Your death in crest announced

As living. To be alive, not dead,
Is to remember always just too late
That living must be done. I wish

That you or I ever could be. The night
As craving wraps its wisps
To every better thought, of what

Could happen in the flesh of someone else,
Not me, the ghost you cannot blink away
& dare not check the time

As prehistoric light streams urgently.
I stare at you, your face that cannot say
A thing but fades with morning.

CAVITY

Dear world we have hit
A cavity, fear reacts
Only, & how daddy does weep. Sugarcunt

Snitches on their darkest desire for
A normal life, o dead village hymnal,
How I long for New York, plump cat

Of desire dark in the gutter, aslant
In the shower, plz Frank can you loan me
A leaf. The pale ale wanker

Of your drippy heart, it is seeping
Thru your pretty nose. I have been told
About angels: a good way to test if your boy

Is an angel, you must snap his feet. You don't
Need feet when you got wings. Break
His feet. Is he sad? Not an angel. It's not

A poem it's a curse. We have shed our own
Skin, we are what's left behind, we watch smoke
Carry on as what we no longer are, can you

Feel that bristle at the tips, how they test
The breeze either way, talk to me about
Mornings. Like seriously I want

An entire life of mornings, to remember & move
Away with the fledgling gait of a promise
From the inability to ever take it back.

PORTRAIT

Families take up too much space
On the pavement, I prefer lewd
Photographs, I prefer degrading

Sex, I prefer not to die or watch
Us be eaten alive. What might it mean for desire
To be a ghost? The sign says bathing

In every shape and form, the gamified heart,
The cop in your pants, the taser
On your tongue. Sometimes in the space

Between wanting & having
You edge history, reactionary in flesh
& haunted by the future, these undead

Hands this cancerous fetus this slogan
You've let slide: strung out on love
Regime with tinnitus, the spooky hole

In the mind that just got real. This ouija board
We play on spells out violence in the form
Of love as penthos, the building fall, delectable

Creep, we twist ourselves into the not yet
Ghosts we have to be, the livid past,
As birds & smoke collapse the sky ahead.

YOU'RE NOT A SUNNY PERSON

You're not a sunny person hard
As concrete in your body cum
On the rafters, chaste at breeze

The sky broken by heat we do
Not fuck. We do with each slow
Glance melt into sex listless

& real, I pick up the trash
Misaligned on the street. Let me be
Your all-gender restroom, your gregarious

Sneeze. Let me be grandiose as I take
Off my clothes. Basically all love is a pact
With death in hushed breath to sit

On your brittle roof. The dress fits
Well. The street is cracked. In your
Arms an easy fall, the numbers unspun

Like a silly wheel. You pull my chest
Apart at the seams, cloaked by trees
Returning, just another lighthouse

Just another shore cornered again
By the grubby thunder, flashes
On fields at dawn in a single note.

DISTRACT

You wake up everyone in the house to tell them
you're going to bed, there's a lighthouse
at the end of history, a beacon that rolls
down stairs. Emptied of pockets the density
of it all becomes pronounced, the word
is sorry, the garden is wet.

We took ourselves out to night, there was
glass in our stories, it changed in the glare. With fire
all flesh burns the same but some more
deservingly, put the key to the car take
the city apart, then our bed is touched
by the sound of a thousand closed windows.

Leavened on couch, miraculous in the face
of nothing, we distend. It is simpler without
looking. It is garish & flayed. You taste like
tomorrow. When the lights crash & the riot
flares the house is unmoved, put our carcass
to rest, take up carrying on.

Freed in crowd the beam of its light is
drowned, we fail at noticing, they have bricks
in their eyes. If we open out the door
has fallen down, I can feel you in reaching,
we are lavished & destroyed. After in morning no one
is there, we knock on the door, we disappear.

SOUTH BRANCIFORTE AVE

They take each other idly by the hand
When crossing roads. All dinosaurs are ghosts
Or birds at the end of the day. Sometimes

It is enough to release a promise
Like a closed fist, an object seen
Again in the dizzy light of another

Arcade, that is warm for admission
& a dozen scurried lisps taking off
In wild screen dusk. Others it is

Not. Early redwoods of the northwest
Graze green flesh against thin full sky.
They shake each other free, liminal & queer

Like a border, like a bathtub collapse,
Like a bedroom slowly recollected
From a dull & brilliant thud. Never have I ever

Said I'm sorry. And who are you? Morning
Twitches like a muscle in taut repose
You see all objects as impossible

& freedom a kind of constrained
Loosening, even if all the dogs
Of daytime in summer coats could never

Restrain you. I am here for collapsing
This thick pillar you call like a body. Born
In a field or again under the full interpretive

Scope of standard california afternoon
That we melted, overheard in conversation
On a dirty bus with jurassic growth

Slapping our fatty bits on the side
That with teeth we have made our mark.
At the end of the day I cook for you

A simple meal, there are planes in the sky
& a dozen forking paths like the shape
Of our genders. It is easier really to rest

In the dirty linen, in the sweat of the grass
& our overgrown bodies, with the cops
On mute, with the dust from this fiery porch

Flung into civic anomaly, the racket
Of bins & a fence in the air & the hungry
Fact of our lives carrying on.

APRIL

Thunder-loosened air, & the lips of the world
at windows we have watched.
Clutching feelings like flowers

for anyone on the street, I want you like Frank
O'Hara wants green, i.e. inconsistently
& confused, where you is interchangeable

with lust for the moment
& green is the world waking up to an instant
of forgetting. To say that love

is to say forgiveness
is to say that nothing matters, or that
everything does, scuttling

thru the eros of difference. Extinguished certainties
linger as props in the hot
mess of identity, & words like ok, & words like it's not,

to settle a moment
from the noise jostling

with the personal for a clear sky,
not visibly but its briefness of silence

in all the burning, & all the opening
& all the not having a clue.

SLEEP

So yes I stumbled, the plantpots are belligerent,
But everyone made it home okay. Through sturdy
Winter out gramophone, brass

In the tips of a clipped wing this old building
Blossomed for, glassy & thick, down pebble & fox
A seaside hill, ghosts in the reverb neon

Poured onto cobble, that they move for
This evening. There is delicacy sometimes
To wait, in clenched note, dispensed in late

Season for catching up with. Sometimes on a beach
At dawn, flexible muscle, indexical & lost, before
This long dissociated motorway the billow

Of tunnel, the bedtime redress. Just the other night
I had a dream in which, within the dream,
One of the figures had previously appeared

In the dream of a lover, present in mine, who alive
Told me the following day they'd never dreamt
This. There is something in this about the way,

Haptic & addled, missing syllable pressed
Against night haze then resented in morning
We longed for, that we could open out.

DUSTIN & COLIN ON FLOOR

for Timothy Thornton

Like really it's the lights that do it put
A glow on put a world inside a world & call
It fleeting watch the bodies crawl with tender
Grasp toward what's warm & not quite dark
Enough to leave your skin behind but still
Unzipped, in sound design in love poem ropes.
I like the square one today. The round ones are
Too well known, in yesterday's blue fade
Away from anywhere but now & losing
Focus. Love is a trope, like a shoreline
I want to let live, I want to let die, a map
Of a map, your fur is the softest, your sibling
Is cautious, some things take a while, I'll remember
You soon, you do not see the coloxdfior, we will not
Sleep again, until Mondays are closed, until after
The ocean & rattling box, until after we've eaten
Every treat & the whole fucking arm, goodnight
Sweetest prince, & your humans, & their names.

FOURTEEN SONNETS IN TRANSITION

1.

The heat leaves the air the shoreline's coast
Goes up in smoke, our city smudged
By street ghost morning flame, at green slope spilled white
Noise blurs & frays, once struck by moon

Light hard in nighttime face. There is no late
Sweet way we haven't made. Now gunfire strips
The sky, unzips its ash & dirt, we line the alleys
Crank the spine, in footnote solace

Soft & bright, you send me flowers
Dressed in gauze I trace the lake, its little glimmers
Cops encompass, all their stupid flashlights splayed.

Now let me with a soft cloth wipe
The blood that dried upon your lip, its quiver, soil & forest spool
In grass that cuts its shape from every grave.

2.

On streets lit up in blue & red the city
Counts its dead.

                    These dreams of killing cops are not enough
You need to pinion them
Alive, distend in catalog
Their tampered breath, & pass the sharpened
Blade from back to front to catch their light, now plunge it deep
Into the lake & pluck like flowers
Their bloody shoes & shields, mark the copse
With flags on fire, so we can keep
The chalkline not the dust.

                    These bags of melted bone, in smear
& window life, at step how rain
Fell the afternoon gone
To grey. Your stupid head on pole, the blubbering neon.
I ask you nicely please for once
Take off their fucking shoes.

3.

Alone or in the morning light clanks
Against the bars. But at a certain angle before evening
Spins its turret, we're a tourist. Now gas me teddy, fuck us up

To spill like petty coins, take an eye to swish
With lukewarm hands, lemon wipe
The gloss away & send your kid to bed, its foot

Lodged in our spine, the future, effigial, his love
Depends on. How will he kiss a face? Who still
Needs feeding? Flowers waking up resist

Their posture, bullet sun again, the shells your cops
In human drag scoop back. Now lachrymatic belt of flames
It's time to leave, we'll gentrify the cheek at wine

Your stupid beard grew from, cut the diaphragm
& douse your precious kid in our fresh wealth.

4.

At massive night crickets chirr
The names apart, in moonstruck distance
Rural chalkline dark unmarks us loosely.

Still warm rock holds
The day's secrets close to flesh, its footprints gauge
The cheek our names have tendered, until morning blunt
Distends its gloss of personhood
That we like cops on fire need to kill, as flowers plucked & shed
These precious violent lives, in dark embrace
Of nothing, yet to hold or give away.

The darkness runs
In siren trill, those precious little lights we chase
From shoes on coast, upon night's peeled display. Just take

Our names, at dog & ghostly bar across the field that moon
Could eat us, let its left light say
In butchered moths what solace yet could pinion.

5.

At scope we hold the dreadful night apart.

                        The light is what your parents did

In lukewarm dreams, the morning sharp

As solace pinions what you get to spill.

                             The sirens trill

In crickets, moths you've butchered, lights left on,

Your parents & their sins. Now turn the country over, press

Restart.

      We cannot fathom you

On every staircase, crumpled sheet across

The freshened sky, a home to find in falling,

Tell them let me in, the cold accosting base of spine

Is neither mine nor yours, this brutal window

Gloss of distant flame encroaching, real bolt

At slip in kitten hands I've got your number. There is no sorry

Word the world can say.

6.

What does it take to let love in. The cops obnoxious
Trill that whittles down benign intent
A little flicker, caramelized in glass
To see you through forever on
The verge of happening
                            --- fuck scuppered mornings
Obsolete in blast incessance, abundant chimney fall
The dull & clodden sidewalk can't live up to, count your steps
                                              back up
& hold them in the slick & sludge, a runway come undone
In bloating breeze. What a fucking state the homing beacon
Up in disarray, to be arrested yet & left to suffer. But in that fickle
Ringing bell, at quay or cracked window, shifting ligaments
The light upside the night & birdsong flies, a glance caught
To hold in loving slack, a bauble in the throat to say a name from
At the pier in whittling flame, the sea inflicting.

7.

The sea inflicted on by english shore, lop off its head
& scorch the prints from hand upon its carcass. Ditzy sore
On runway watched my ppl kill
Their friends to live, like cops
Open interpret, carry what you need, a scene
That feeds itself what it could vomit. Chase the bug away
We make it in the places landlords weep, your parents
Pay your rent, that's nice, let's hope you live
A happy life.
          In open windows light eclipses
Shitty shores, on ocean floating
Back toward, a place to sharpen knives from desperate chatter,
                        says whatever's left
Is where to make some life we can believe in. Fuck your industry
& what you tell yourself to sleep. On cops as base
& landlord blood infused we season poets
Little whittled herbs, your bay leaf title
No one cares, good luck w that promotion.

8.

Belated rain drops its little hope

           Along the block, the sound of names

Your life away, in death for so long

           We have lived as if with means to speak, or sirens fade

A shoreline in reverse, to say

With wonder unencumbered for a moment on your lips you love

The stars.

        Is it too much to ask

           For something we could never have? Or cop spun off

In dandelion slain, from fire escape, unwhittled bell

         Of city stripped to comic flame

A pool of blood blossoms, rip the guts out, stand to gain— a stake

    On feral ground, laid out in plastic, up sunset deranged

      The mask removes its face

         To show us in disdain what rots & flays,

All edges uncontained, the coast a warning.

9.

Now it's time to pin the ashes on the wind
& let them spin, a shape unmade
Cannot be held until, given away, that truncheon of a spine
At buckle breaks, & stumped in leaves the sun you struck

A prayer to every morning pukes new flame.
                                        The city out
The window scuppered teeth, a mouth they tried to make
Obey from every edge & slick escape, with tongue in wave
An earthquake, please, we need it, dream & brick.
                                        Then once again
That lip, the glassy condo weep
To liquid floor, you hold me up
& reaching, stretch of ash, its treetip glimpse

We spell out penthos screaming
Fresh & lava, see the water wake
With corpses whittled, shields scrubbed clean to break.

10.

A heart, an angel, morning, coast at rock, pan up thru street
Unshielded light, the gutted air, so cheap to breathe, for once
& what the fuck do we do now. The ghosts at glass

Who slice a dozen futures every angle opened, hold on
To the shoreline, fists of grass, the drowning steam, a mouth
Its scar of speech, inside a rumbling, bar & key, our name

A lonely warrant left to rest. There is no late feat performed
Apart these roots, they twitch & cannot state the lung
We ask for, gills on sky & blood bled out the bay. Just take

Me home. The trees at chalkline, warnings unerased, this gleam
Of pockets. What else is left, what murder to invent, or seam
To plunder. Now breathing, free, no shield at light, the street

A rock, an angel, tired heart. What open whim or candle unallayed. Bones
& fingers, flowers, blue & red. Spell on tongue, a hex, awake the dead.

11.

Day heat sinks slow & lingering
To night. On streets too steep to pay
Rain falls, they've left so many

Bodies on the road, in acrid gist
Of wanting to be whole. Tonight
They're gone in chalkline dust,

A forming lake & life made small,
By the light water shreds.
There are no cops as we reach out

Across the battered lake, & living heat
Depleted sells for free its stench, a brittle love,
A window washed to sand — that open door

The forest never named; a wake
That rips the nails from the stage.

12.

Our night car writes the road away
In light & water splays, fire in the distance
Burning out.

            There is no clean escape
To make, at rented peace trees bend
To hold their shape, & sunset finally breaks.

But what a hand to hold inside a morning on the run
We wait for stars, pacific breeze squashed
& dark, the coast a broken magnet.

                      You let me go
At clearing, the need for you, frantic
Cityless gleam, no end to hide from.

                       & back
Home another name, sirens mute, our faces
In the mirror's sliced lake, a lifting smog, sun
Cracked against the glass & sluicing down
What's left ajar, the splinter of a promise.

13.

Light breaks thru the whittled rooms.

At brittle cop char departure shapes,

We hold in glassy pose, suspiciously

A house against the odds.

                      Now step inside

Its empty space, what name could hold this eager weight

Or taste its texture, loosen a self

& not burn up on sight?

                          Birdsong dresses night wound in lake shreds,

Echoed steps in fight or flight

Scatter like seed.

                In breath aflame no voice to say

I want survival, give me life that doesn't hurt,

Or hurts with meaning. With fire it could go

Either way. Our city wilting like a map,

We stack the bones in sound

& crush to chalk.

14.

At the end of the world the world begins again
In wreckage sharpening knives beside the lake.
There is no getting clean. A good cop is nothing
But a hollow print unearthed & cast back
Into the ashes of when fire was a promise
With no name. You take your shoes off & they
Are swallowed. You hope the trash will disappear
With morning. The air cannot survive
Some forms of hope.
                              In chalk & smoke desire becomes
The ghost its pull was made from, earth & bone
Still holding pose, release the dead as silent chorus
Into evening rain. There is no getting clean.
                              At waterside
With sharpened knives
The world begins again.

AMBIVALENCE (AN AMERICAN LYRIC)

1.

After catastrophe in its middle
We need a password for the road.

Another cabin several trees
Down holds enemies, before

The freeway's cratered promise
Or fire climbs the static, city

At its favorite silhouette.
Valley flattens miles away the state

No longer green, children trapped
At home & oil-drunk earth.

Left at light the streets an empty
Parking lot, your cop alone

At cold coffee, no one left
To chase or carve a name

Just rope or going on. & sun, tepid,
Little rustling leaves

2.

Whoever thought to name a ghost hope
You must begrudge them, little children
Of your flung ideas. We left behind our voices

On the street, their petty carvings, notches
Made upon the trunk of what a life cannot
Live up to, dizzy sparkler halo. & in the sound

Electric-whetted engine many centuries
At tangle, grabby hands & squashed lament.
I watch your eyes distorted by the road.

Now parents of America bring your dead
The overdosed & left alone. At night for fire
Wood is wet we hammer out a pattern

Of what would, in better lighting, have been told.
These lovely ruins, this bitter fickle longing
Unexpired. & sunlight drops its axe right thru our bed.

3.

Alight at night the situation seems more liminal.

I want to say an open pier awaits us.

                              But even if we could become

What we have never been

A promise must remain something

To anchor.

               & in the morning

Floods & engines scream, huffy embers

Begging to be stomped or broken in.

4.

At mountain great private silent
Heart of paranoia, in wind chimes
& sun-sharpened snow.
            That tight chest accessory
Worn under your words spilled
Onto forest floor & into glass.
The cops here take the shape of fear
Unseen, a certain glance or hidden hand.
But as the snow melts & night collapses all that fell
Finds its way into the pressing stream, footsteps in the crosshairs
Where the quiet never leaves.

5.

What could labor ever do beside this carrying on.
The tercets of your hair & held blue breath. How crazy
That the sun could even reach here, high or not.
No windows left to dash or run away from. Now when
The wood is chopped & all this life has been reset, we see
What could have been in branch-lit gleam.

6.

Gunpowder twig your try to see through
What's not there, a broken clock
& pathways winding fickle.
                         Someone told you
Never let me go. The harness of a hope inside
An endless precipice, anxiety that melts the paint
Before you've turned away.
                         Oh isn't it so lovely
To be known, this land of dust kicked up by trucks
& other miscreants of distant friendship.

7.

Now all my favorite writers, in the end, did not exist
& yet we tried. A leaf is still a leaf when footprints
Lie. To want to go out to the lake that stayed behind
Another far off place. Mostly I just want you to survive.

8.

The promise held its moment as a way to let it pass
Slowly. This is where the lives were built & jobs. A Tory
Always infiltrates your heart. Such hostage love to future
Where from distance you can safely now have been there.
Your lips get smaller when you're mad. What we're really wanting
Through it all is it to stop. & then an afternoon
Like this that never ends, inimitable sun to pin
The whole fragile thing in place, its bludgeon
& caress, where nothing even is to need to be.

9.

The cabin has outlived so many we have never met. & night as well
Outlives us every day. Never enough words to say
For even these small things, that still confuse us.

The violent hymns in tree & sunlight holding ground,
Where'd you meet the dead today whose were they.
A friend in photo holds us for a moment as the snow

That will not budge or cede the distance between friend
& enemy. Where are the knives we need & how to use them.
Carved in bullets sky has fixed its pins & laid us down

To lie & keep on trying. At dark the deer eyes like tasers,
Chainsaw echoes in the sneaky breeze. The creaking wood,
A missing witness, watch its light extinguish into space.

10.

Light rises like exhausted smoke
Into another thick & depthless night

Left behind. You ran around a childhood
Shootout, sumps & pluming rust. Debt

& scattered dollars in a city on the make.
The road back down is crabs & buckets

Lapsed refineries & sundried billboards.
What have we been doing with our lives.

The rearview cop who disappears in glints
Lodged in your spine, a freeway & a fire

In the cove. & by the outhouse promises
Of knives. There's only so much skin we have

To shed for better longing or remorse. You take me
Where the skyline disappears, & what we have, to say,

Is only something once we overheard. Half stuck
& half in motion as the sirens churn & bleed

We leave our faces to the silence, cut the lights
& join the blaze. Whatever's left is nothing yet to say.

GREEN

I am writing this to you from a perpetually compromised state
of unfixed intent. That is not news, the world etc., but in some
nebulous kingdom where decay has taken over, on a beach say,
algaeic dream, stench seen above from ghost hotel, fickle little
spool, you make a flame in the now slight doorway light.

A boat and a lake, memory of blue, & the flitting cruelties of
green. I cannot read the day. Ambivalence borne. The light of a
thousand dying lights, at different times, bloodpool, a walk simply
in the park, we speak of ducks, the leash the lash, & bodies press
as pink collapsed & bled, the plywood wincing.

This cannot be the end you say in flames. Spies in the night, spies
at tower, fingernails & folding, scattered cat, face slashed back
behind the curtains, a dream of cobblestone & broken grid, we
reach the ocean window dashing stars & continental drift, your
doorway match our whispers brushing into.

& out the window into leaves their fading dream of green.
Some buttress fed, wound up in modem screech, with city
buzzing, plump & new, each falling, night on charge. Our broken
phonebooth hope, accosted by the memory of air outside the
bar, recurring plunge, alleys all askew & cop torch butchering the
asphalt.

A pinch of salt, reality is sluggish, pick her up they're coming, what's the time. You dash onto the street we hit the foliage, at bush this evening's shreds, hueless & warm, of skin & whittled clothing, the whole world drowning in our damp extended hands & then reborn, it's gone, the morning's perilous light, confused & green

ACKNOWLEDGEMENTS

The poems in this collection were written in, and are to some extent about, the following locations: Santa Cruz, Portland, San Francisco, Calistoga, Camp Nelson, and England. Thank you to Ruby Piper, without whom I would never have been in many of those places. Special thanks to Timothy Thornton for the company, yaps, rants, and many years of being the most careful, generous, and supportive reader anyone could hope for. Thank you to Richard Porter and Andrew McMillan for the ongoing support and encouragement. Thanks to Aaron Kent and Andre Bagoo at Broken Sleep for the feedback and for giving this book a home!

Versions of 'Lighthouse Field,' 'On Accuracy,' 'King Curtis,' 'Torque,' 'Cavity,' 'Portrait,' 'You're Not a Sunny Person,' 'Distract,' 'South Branciforte Avenue,' 'April,' 'Sleep,' and 'Dustin & Colin On Floor' were previously published as part of *Diametric Fist Tender* (Pilot Press, 2020). 'On Accuracy' was included in *100 Queer Poems* (Vintage, 2022). Sections 1-4 of 'Fourteen Sonnets in Transition' appeared in *Datableed*.

LAY OUT YOUR UNREST

Adelheid Fischer

SCIENCE OF SEEING

Essays on Nature from
Zygote Quarterly

ZQ BOOKS

ZQ Books
Calgary, Canada
© Adelheid Fischer 2017

Print
ISBN 978-1-7750150-0-0

Ebook
ISBN 978-1-7750150-1-7

To biologist Chel Anderson, who introduced me to the wonders of blue-spotted salamanders, floating bogs, star-nosed moles and so much more.

"We do a lot of looking: we look through lenses, telescopes, television tubes. Our looking is perfected every day—but we see less and less. Never has it been more urgent to speak of seeing."

From *The Zen of Seeing* by Frederick Franck

CONTENTS

FOREWORD

I ONCE WATCHED HERBERT WAITE, A MATERIAL SCI-entist at UC Santa Barbara, get swept off a rock jetty by an errant wave. Before I could yell for help, he corked up, caught a swell, and hoisted himself back onto the black, glistening boulders, careful not to disturb the blue mussels he'd come to study. He waved I'm OK, squeezed the surf from his curly beard and windshield-wipered his glasses to make me laugh. For the next few hours, he was gone, focused intently on the bed of swaying mussels before him.

How you watch says everything about what you will notice. Herb Waite watches mussels (*Mytilus edulis*) to learn *from* them, not just *about* them, and for more than 30 years, his worshipful vigil has yielded incredible insights: a glue that cures underwater, a tethering thread called byssus that's stiff at one end and rubbery at the other (functional gradients!) and a transparent sheath that protects the byssus from bacteria and saltwater. In a process called biomimicry, inventors have mimicked the mussel's superpowers to create a form-aldehyde-free plywood glue, suture-free wound closures and a heavy-metal-pollution-detection device.

Learning *from* an organism requires a suspension of what you think you know, and a Goethe-like willingness to be taught. The last time I visited Herb, he told me his latest lesson from byssus threads had nothing to do with materials science.

One day at high tide, he watched a predatory periwinkle snail drill into the shell of a submerged mussel. Seconds later, he was flabbergasted to see dozens and dozens of mussels jettison their byssus and float away, like a platoon of underwater balloons. He was startled by how fast the communiqué spread. Months of subsequent study revealed that when a mussel is attacked, it immediately yanks on its byssus, alerting neighbors who yank on their byssus, and so on. The Paul Revere call spreads in concentric waves, allowing the rest of the colony to escape.

Because of how he watches, Waite learned that byssus is both a wondrous material and a vital communication device. He reminds us that the lessons of nature's technologies are best understood in context, and the context for mussels, as for humans, is community.

When biomimics watch, they break from the traditions that have defined nature study. Of the ten or more million possible species, we know the names of only a million and a half, and very little is known about the species that aren't commercially, recreationally or medically of interest to us. Our libraries are filled with accounts of organisms that we domesticate and farm, those we hunt for sport or medicine and those we fear and hope to eradicate.

Biomimicry changes that, because it reminds us that our planet-mates have far more to offer than their caloric count or their ability to cause or cure disease. Their evolved answer to the question "How shall we live here?" is worth staying in the ocean for, worth being swept away by waves.

Adelheid Fischer dives into wildernesses large and small to show us the twinned lives of organisms and the researchers patient enough to study them in the field. Hers is a reverential, yet practical reportage that offers solace for the modern heart and a rare hope: If these organisms can live so competently in their places, perhaps we can too. Once you meet the stars of these essays—outrageously tactile moles, volcano-healing spiders, old-growth forests that hide in plain sight and deserts that sparkle at dawn—you'll never watch nor see the natural world in the same way again. Adelheid's singular voice will make you feel you have stumbled upon a memento box filled with thank you notes for all the natural world has given her. Welcome to the poetry of gratitude.

Janine Benyus
Montana, 2017

PREFACE

WE ARE PROUD TO BRING YOU THE FIRST IN A SERIES
of special collections selected from the digital
pages of ZQ magazine. Our purpose is to respond
to our readers' many requests for the publica-
tion of thematic writings; to give these writings
their "own space" as it were, so that they can be
enjoyed as tangible bodies of work or used as tools
for teaching and study. Later editions will contain
case studies and professional techniques and
strategies.

The decision to launch this series with the work
of Adelheid Fischer was an easy one. Our most
popular writer and an author in her own right,
Adelheid captures the essence of our subject: the
wonder at nature's endless gifts and admiration
for the men and women who study it for our
common good. Tromping across the slopes of the
Mount St. Helens volcano, or in a listening crouch
in the night-time desert or peering into an ephem-
eral pool, she has the ability to make us all see
more clearly. Her zeal for life, perseverance on the
trail and reverence for nature are infectious and
come alive in the pages you are about to enjoy.

Tom McKeag & the ZQ editors

ACKNOWLEDGEMENTS

SPECIAL THANKS TO THE BIOMIMICRY CENTER AT Arizona State University which supported the research and writing of these essays.

My deep thanks and admiration also go to the editors of *Zygote Quarterly*: Marjan Eggermont, Tom McKeag and Norbert Hoeller. I stand in awe of your ambition, professionalism and hard work in making *ZQ* such a smart and sumptuous entré to the inspiration of the natural world.

Most of all, I would like to thank the scientists profiled in this book who set aside time for interviews and allowed me to tag along with them up mountain streams, along the foot of volcanos, through ponderosa-pine forests and Sonoran and red-rock deserts. Some of my finest hours were spent in your company: Kate Boersma, Rod Crawford, Charlie Crisafulli, Jim Davis, Laurence Garvie, Tim Graham, Erick Greene, Britné Hackett, Wendy Hodgson and Doug Larson. May you and your organisms live long and prosper!

1

THERE ARE NO
STRANGERS IN
THE WORLD

I PULL UP A CHAIR NEXT TO THE LOW WALL THAT separates my yard from South Mountain, a desert preserve of nearly 17,000 acres near the southern edge of the City of Phoenix. Out from the creosote thickets flies a tiny buff-brown bird. Verdin. Although I've seen hundreds of these desert dwellers, which are as common in the city as they are in wilder parts of the Sonoran Desert, they'll still get a rise from my binoculars. From afar, verdins are just another LBJ (which in birdwatching parlance means "little brown job"). A closer look, however, reveals a flush of gold that spreads from face to crown like the soft, seamless glow in the desert sky just after a clear sunset. Equally extraordinary, but harder to spot, are crimson epaulets on each shoulder. Since these jittery birds never hold still for long, following them with binoculars is likely to give me a mild case of motion sickness. Today is no exception. The verdin beelines into the tall wands of an ocotillo and, clutching one in each claw, begins to pump the air until the branches whipsaw in the wind. He lets fly his customary greeting, a sharp two- and three-note command that sounds like a drill sergeant in a Buddhist boot camp. "Be here. Be here NOW!"

Where is "here"? Where is "now"? I've posed these questions to myself daily, ever since the night in 2005, when my husband of twenty-five years woke up in a coughing fit, mumbled a few incoherent words and died as I watched. In less than a minute, the man who was as essential to me as breath and bread, gravity and water, air, sunlight and birdsong, simply disappeared. I became a stranger to the world.

For nearly a year, I hardly strayed from my backyard, leaving only to buy groceries, to meet friends or to hike a steep trail in South Mountain to a summit where I could look out for tens of miles in every direction, a temporary furlough from the dark, cramped halls of grief. Some evolutionary psychologists have speculated that our species often responds to loss with a predictable complex of encoded feelings and behaviors. Sadness and its attendant lethargy, for example, are protective since, in prehistoric times, they kept us close to home and away from the kind of distracted wandering that was likely to make us easy prey for hungry lions or, in modern times, from mindlessly stepping off the curb into oncoming traffic. By slowing us down and keeping us close, sadness may be psychologically adaptive as well, since by zapping our energy "it enforces a kind of reflective retreat from life's busy pursuits," observes behavioral science writer Daniel Goleman, "and leaves us in a suspended state to mourn the loss, mull over its meaning, and, finally, make the psychological adjustments and new plans that will allow our lives to continue."

For biophiliacs like me, there can be no new plans, no new meaning-making, no new life stories that aren't as densely populated with the winged, the four-legged or chitin-coated kind as they are with people. As such, I was lucky to be living in the Sonoran Desert, the most biologically diverse of the North American deserts. Guides appeared almost daily with their own stories of transformative journeys and fantastical life histories. It was as if the plants and animals in my backyard were leaving a breadcrumb trail across the abyss that led to a reconnection with life. Fellow biophiliac Barbara Kingsolver describes this process in the conclusion of her essay "High Tide in Tucson." "In my own worst seasons," she writes, "I've come back from the colorless world of despair by forcing myself to look hard, for a long time, at a single glorious thing: a flame of red geranium outside my bedroom window. And then another: my daughter in a yellow dress. And another: the perfect outline of a full, dark sphere behind the crescent moon. Until I learned to be in love with my life again. Like a stroke victim retraining new parts of the brain to grasp lost skills, I have taught myself joy, over and over again."

Among the first to penetrate my quarantine of mourning with offerings of joy were the bees that favored the butterscotch blooms of Superstition mallow next to my kitchen window. Tucson entomologist Stephen Buchmann pointed out that my visitors were undoubtedly members of the genus *Diadasia*, a solitary, ground-nesting bee native to the Sonoran Desert. On warm afternoons, they would dive into the heart of the flowers, kneading their pollen-packed stores for hours without letup. But as the sun went down and temperatures cooled, they would suddenly cease and collapse onto their plush stamen beds, like a weary baker at the close of his workday simply tipping over to sleep in a great vat of dough. The petals then slowly closed around the food-comatose bees, sheltering them in tiny hammocks where they could sleep, safe and warm. On stormy nights, I'd sometimes walk out in the dark to check on the mallows, smiling as the shuttered blooms gently rocked in the breeze. The next day, long after the flower petals had reopened in the sun, I'd find that many of the bees were still asleep, like teenagers tangled in bedsheets at high noon. Peering at them through a magnifying glass, their bristled body hairs patchy with gold dust, I'd gently nudge their drowsy backs with my finger. "Dudes, sleepyheads," I'd whisper. "Time's a-wasting. Chop-chop."

And then there were the odd two years when late-season summer rains triggered an irruption of the larvae of white-lined sphinx moths. Tens of thousands of yellow- and black-striped caterpillars inched down from the mountain summits. Like the marauding hordes from the Dark Ages (I half expected to hear the stomp of spears and clang of chainmail), they overtopped my back wall in droves, falling with an audible "plop" into the writhing mass of their cousins on the other side. They fanned out into the neighborhoods with a kind of blind determination, their inner compasses set in the unwavering direction of south. The invasion lasted for days and ceased as abruptly as it began. The greasy stains on the roads and sidewalks where the plump caterpillars crossed paths with cars and footfall remained the only evidence of their great, mysterious passing.

And then there were the magical couplings of spring, when the clusters of matchstick-red buds at the tips of the ocotillos burst into flames of open flowers. Orioles suddenly appeared, as if conjured from their long migrations north, to prick the blooms and drain them of their nectar. Or the first hot morning in late spring when the rise of a few degrees on the thermometer seemed to cause white-winged doves to drop from the sky. "Koo-koo ka-choo," they called on cue, sounding none the worse for the wear of having trailed the great spine of the Sierra Madres in Mexico to feast on the flowers and fruit of the saguaro cactus, here on their summer breeding grounds in the Sonoran Desert.

It wasn't until I began to study biomimicry, though, that I gained a kind of genealogical framework for understanding—and not simply cherishing—this kinship with life. In 2007, I traveled to the Front Range of the Rockies for a weeklong training workshop hosted by the Biomimicry Guild. We had been ticking through a list of what guild biologists call Life's Principles (general rules by which nature operates and against which designers can test the overall fitness of their solutions) when we got to one now-familiar entry: "Nature Uses Simple Common Building Blocks." DNA, for example. The only nonbiologist in the group, I found myself stumbling through my foggy memory of Biology 101. I recalled that DNA, the fundamental script of life's operating manual, comprises a mere four nucleotides: guanine, adenine, thymine and cytosine. Four, I suddenly realized! Just four! It was as if blood began to pump through the veins of the rote learning of my high school days and insight took flight from the page: all living things are cut from the same chemical cloth! The commonalities were nothing short of astounding: we share 96 percent of our genes with chimpanzees; 97.5 percent with mice; nearly 60 percent with fruit flies; and 26 percent with yeasts. It was my first epiphany. My second came when I realized that plant and animal adaptations—working solutions to the challenges that life presents— are not fixed and immutable in space and time. We are all drawn and erased and redrawn by the same restless, creative life force. We are all in a constant state of becoming—together.

In his Pulitzer Prize-winning book, *The Beak of the Finch*, Jonathan Weiner writes about this continual state of realignment, about life's propensity for making ongoing course corrections, as it is expressed in the finches in the Galapagos Islands. "The original meaning of the word evolution—the unrolling of a scroll—suggested a metamorphosis, as of moths or beetles or butterflies," Weiner writes. "But the insects' metamorphosis has a conclusion, a finished adult form. The Darwinian view of evolution shows that the unrolling scroll is always being written, inscribed as it unrolls. The letters are composed by the hand of the moment, by the circumstances of the day itself. We are not completed as we stand, this is not our final stage. There can be no finished form for us or for anything else alive...." For me this was biomimicry's most startling, most enduring lesson: we are the kin of living things, deep into the molecular recesses of our being. We are never alone, never strangers, in the world.

If scientists ever get around to sequencing the genome of *Diadasia*, perhaps I will have hard evidence for what I already know: that solitary bees and the solitary writers who love them wake to labor in sisterhood in the same generative light of creation. "Whoever you are," writes Mary Oliver in her poem "Wild Geese,"

> *"no matter how lonely,*
> *the world offers itself to your imagination,*
> *calls to you like the wild geese, harsh and*
> *exciting—*
> *over and over announcing your place*
> *in the family of things."*

2

HIDING IN FULL VIEW

You can observe a lot just by watching.
                Yogi Berra, renowned baseball player
                            and folk philosopher

The true journey of discovery consists not in seek-ing new landscapes but in having fresh eyes.
                                    Marcel Proust

SEVERAL YEARS AGO, WHILE RESEARCHING THE ecology of Great Lakes forests, I came across some research that stopped me in my tracks.

It all started with a Canadian rock climber named Steven Spring. In the 1980s Spring would spend hours dangling from ropes along the cliffs of the Niagara Escarpment, the limestone edge of an ancient seabed that slices across much of the Upper Great Lakes region. From time to time, the climber and avid naturalist would pause on his adventures to examine the cliff edge up close. From a distance, the 100-foot-tall façade appeared sheer and largely featureless. When viewed at arm's length, however, the rock wall broke into a complex puzzle of ledges, runways and alcoves that teemed with life: snails, snakes, centipedes and bobcats as well as rare plant species, some of which have held their ground in these vertical outposts since the last glaciation. What really captured Spring's attention, though—and his imagination—were the miniature white cedars that had sunk their gnarly, bird-claw roots deep into empty crevices or clutched at what appeared to be nothing more than bare rock. With little or no soils in which to root, how did these bonsai-like trees survive?

•

In 1985 Spring began scouting for a project for his master's thesis. He wandered into the research lab of Dr. Douglas Larson, a botanist at the University of Guelph, Ontario. Larson, a lichenologist, had already attracted a cluster of students who were interested in the ecology of tough places. Spring's curiosity about the tiny trees had finally found a home. Larson's league of the like-minded coalesced into what became known as the Cliff Ecology Research Group. From the Niagara Escarpment, the group's research spread out to far-flung locations throughout the eastern U.S. and Europe. Before long, the news from Larson's lab began making science headlines.

It turns out that just about everywhere they went, the Cliff Ecology Research Group discovered ecological goldmines that were hiding in plain sight. Segments of the Niagara Escarpment, for example, could be seen from downtown Toronto, then a city of some two million people, and yet no one had even so much as bothered to take a census of their extraordinary inhabitants. "Vertical cliff ecosystems were completely overlooked by ecologists because they appeared to be hostile, lifeless and seemingly impossible to sample. Indeed they do not even show up on the most detailed aerial photographs," wrote Larson and his colleagues, Peter Kelly and Ute Matthes-Sears, in Encyclopaedia Britannica's 1995 *Science Yearbook*. Even world-famous cliffs like Gibraltar and Dover, they observed, which long had been the stuff of postcards and insurance logos, "have attracted no scientific inquiry."

For every ounce of investigative effort in places like the Niagara Escarpment, the researchers seemed to reap a tenfold reward. Initial surveys, for example, yielded an impressive tally of invertebrate species. An unexpected bonus was the extraordinary species diversity of the cliff's snail populations. The scientists also discovered startling clues to the region's paleo history which suggested that the cliff ecosystem once had—and continues to maintain—greater affinities with the tundra than with the temperate, sugar maple-dominated forest that surrounds it today. Among the tantalizing remnants of times gone by were the bones of an extinct species of pika. Not all the glacial holdovers were fossils, however. Of the 25 or so living species of herbaceous plants that the researchers documented, five were found to be members of species that occur more commonly in the Arctic. These were the descendants of plant communities that once had hunkered under the frigid katabatic winds of the Wisconsin ice sheet and still persisted in place on the steep cliff walls.

The biggest surprise of all came in some of the escarpment's small packages—the cliff's elfin trees. Temperature readings showed that they endured extremes of 110 degrees in summer to minus 20 degrees in winter. Many had grown bent and crabbed under the inexorable pull of gravity. Some of them seemed to defy gravity altogether by corkscrewing horizontally out of the rock. How did they survive?

A closer examination revealed a suite of extraordinary adaptations. For starters, the roots of the cliff-edge trees were covered in mycorrhizal fungi. These organisms are adept at exploiting the "solution hollows" in the rock surface, tiny dimples that capture soil and moisture, to scavenge precious resources like phosphorus, nitrogen and water. The root fungi share this harvest with their host trees in exchange for the carbohydrates they produce through photosynthesis. Thanks to mice and other animals, fungal spores are seeded widely in feces throughout the cliff ecosystem.

This nutrient-swapping arrangement between trees and mycorrhizae occurs commonly in other kinds of plant communities so it was not entirely groundbreaking news. Another kind of ecological partnership did grab headlines, however. The researchers suspected that the tiny trees might have been able to take advantage of a far more unusual source of nutrients: those produced by organisms that live inside the rock itself.

·

From Antarctica to the deserts of the Middle East and American Southwest, scientists have published sporadic reports of communities of algae, lichen and fungi that live within solid rock. They're known as cryptoendolithic ("hidden inside rock") organisms. Researchers speculate that the harsh conditions of their environments drove them "indoors" to find shelter from the elements. Among the most important are the algae, especially those known as cyanobacteria, which are able to transmute atmospheric nitrogen into a form that plants can utilize. No one had documented the existence of these cryptoendoliths in southern Ontario until the cliff-ecology researchers whacked a few chunks of rock from the cliff face and discovered, just beneath the surface, a thriving community of organisms arrayed in narrow, green bands. How the nutrients that are produced by these secretive societies make their way into the cliff environment remains something of a mystery but "they are very likely contributing significant amounts of nitrogen compounds to the cliff ecosystems and are probably indirectly fertilizing the trees at a rate just high enough to keep them and the whole ecosystem alive," Larson and his colleagues write.

The most intriguing news of all, however, came after Larson's colleague, Peter Kelly, conducted dendrological tests on the miniature cedars. It was no easy task. To date trees, scientists commonly carry out a harmless procedure in which they core a plug from a tree trunk and count its rings. But the morphology of cliff-edge trees complicates this straightforward task. That's because 90 percent of them have roots and trunks that ripple over the rock face and attach in multiple places, forming splayed, asymmetrical growth patterns much like the disorderly locks on the head of Medusa.

These roots are extremely vulnerable in the cliff environment. During its lifetime, a tree will endure traumatic root loss about ten times as roots are dislodged or exposed by disturbances such as falling rocks or ice buildup. Whether on an unstable cliff face or in a quiescent swamp, cedars have, nonetheless, developed clever strategies for coping with the vagaries of this world. The roots operate independently of one another, each funneling water and nutrients to its own part of the tree stem. "It's a clever system," Larson observes. "If a rock gives way and detaches a root, only the portion of the trunk that was connected to that specific root will die." As such, he says, each individual tree "is actually behaving as a population of independent parts rather than as an integrated being."

The cedars' ingenious modes of gathering resources and safeguarding their distributed delivery channels have served these trees well. Overlooked by loggers and spared by wildfires, the trees have attained ripe old ages. Surveys by Larson and his colleagues showed that trees ranging between 300 and 800 years of age are common on the escarpment. Some are well over 1,000 years old. One dead tree that was discovered at the base of the cliff near Toronto was nearly 1,900 years old before it toppled to the ground! Common to all of them was their small stature. Even the oldest trees measured only about 10 feet high and less than 12 inches in diameter.

This was the most unexpected and wonderful discovery of all: in full view of factories and farm fields, surrounded by city streets and second- and third-growth woodlots was an old-growth forest. "The exposed cliffs of the Niagara Escarpment—the cliffs thought by some people to be 'barren' or 'lifeless'—actually supported the oldest and most undisturbed forest ecosystem in eastern North America," wrote Larson and his colleagues.

The potential for this kind of paradigm-busting discovery abounds, the scientists conclude. "What is most significant," they write, "is that by studying a place and by asking questions that have been ignored or avoided by others, researchers can make discoveries that are both globally important and exciting. Similar opportunities exist everywhere in the scientific landscape."

3

JEWELS OF THE DESERT

LAURENCE GARVIE MAKES A LEFT TURN OFF A DIRT road, crosses a line of railroad tracks and pulls over into a makeshift clearing in Saguaro National Monument. I reach instinctively for my hat, water bottle and sunglasses as we step out of his truck, blinking in the desert's hard white light one late morning in June. Although the site is less than two hours south of his office on the Tempe campus of Arizona State University, Garvie may as well be on another planet. As curator of the Center for Meteorite Studies at ASU, the world's largest university-based meteorite collection, he spends most of his working hours in a hushed, humidity-controlled room that is lined floor to ceiling with small drawers. They contain more than 30,000 extraterrestrial rock specimens that have hurtled to Earth from places as far away as the asteroid belt. An expert in electron microscopy, Garvie peers into their mineral structures for clues to the formation of the Solar System.

Garvie is as perfectly at ease in the desert heat as he is in the cool, dim recesses of his ASU lab. In his spare time, the self-described desert rat can be found roaming the remote reaches of the Sonoran Desert—but not, as you might suspect, with his nose to the ground in search of meteorites. He studies the structure of cactus spines or listens to beetles rasping the woody hollows of a dead palo verde tree or picks through the charred remains of a mesquite after a rare wildfire. These are the kinds of goings-on in the desert that most people pass again and again with hardly a glance. For Garvie, however, they are every bit as intriguing as the mysterious mineral debris that rains down from outer space.

"Look at that spider," he points out as we trudge down a wash to the shade of a mesquite tree for lunch. "We haven't had rain in two months. How does it survive?"

To accompany Garvie on a walk in the desert is to witness what it means to care about a place, as defined by the deep meaning of the word's Old English root, *cearu*, which means to guard or watch, "to trouble oneself." Simply paying attention to the particulars of the world and taking the trouble to find out more about them have led Garvie to a whole grab bag of discoveries, many of which are new to science. On one desert outing in 1998, for example, he came across a small prehistoric potsherd covered by several different kinds of lichens. He took the specimen to his ASU colleagues, lichenologists Tom Nash and Matthias Schultz, who determined that one of them was the first known occurrence of that particular species in the U.S. On another trip, Garvie pocketed a sample of a large and lumpy black lichen that he discovered growing on an outcrop of limestone, a type of rock that is not commonly exposed in the Sonoran Desert. Nash and Schultz declared it to be a whole new species. A few years ago Garvie published a paper in a botanical journal, becoming the first to describe how, as saguaros age, the structure of their spine clusters changes dramatically, from formidable, downward-facing spikes when the cactuses are small to a more starburst-like pattern in their later years. "It's not some great scientific discovery," he observes. "For me, it was just a little puzzle that I'd seen for years."

Arguably some of Garvie's most exciting desert adventures have led him to explore the afterlife of saguaros, the towering sentinels of the desert that can grow to 60 feet or more and reach grand old ages of 200 years. As they near the end of their lives, these desert elders commonly are felled by a systemic disease in which fungi and bacteria attack the plant's moist inner tissues. A telltale sign of infection is the weeping of a ripe-smelling black liquid from openings in the saguaro's skin. Once the disease spreads, the plant turns into what Garvie calls a "fetid bag of goo" that can be easily downed by a strong wind.

Yet saguaros are as important to desert wildlife in death as they are in life. The towering cactuses are like gigantic sponges, their internal tissues saturated with up to 90 percent water. When they are toppled, they become an "organic moist soup that's teeming with life," he observes, adding that in the immediate aftermath of death, "the whole thing is moving, heaving with bugs, worms, and all sorts of microorganisms. It's quite exciting."

Scientists at the University of Arizona have conducted extensive postmortems of freshly toppled saguaros. In one cubic foot of a rotting saguaro, they catalogued 413 arthropods including beetles in both adult and larval stages, larval flies, pseudoscorpions, and mites. Some of them occur only in dead saguaros.

But when Garvie tore off a chunk of the rotting cactus, the mineralogist found more than biological treasures. "It was almost like a geode," he explains. "The insides sparkled in the sun from all the new crystals that had formed." But even more startling discoveries awaited Garvie when he took the glassy jewels back to his lab. The results were confounding. "I looked at my data and said, What on earth is this?" he recalls. His finds included rare, magnesium-bearing crystals with such exotic sounding names as lansfordite, glushinskite and nesquehonite (which has been located in mines and caves and is a common weathering product of Antarctic meteorites). Others rarely occurred in deserts. At least half a dozen additional crystals, he observes, were new to science.

These exotic crystals, however, form only when the saguaro's putrefying pockets are moist, quickly disintegrating as conditions dry out. Other minerals—with equally strange and fascinating life stories—linger long after the plant's tissues have disappeared. As a newcomer to the Sonoran Desert in the 1990s, Garvie noticed chunks of a bone-colored material, as light and porous as pumice, heaped around the exposed wooden ribs of saguaro skeleton, the last of the plant's remains to decompose. "I remember collecting a piece after a year or so. It sat on my desk for another year. One day I had a few minutes and I subjected it to powder X-ray diffraction [a method geologists use to identify minerals]," Garvie recalls. Much to his surprise, the material was monohydrocalcite (also known as hydrated calcium carbonate). The last place Garvie expected to find this relatively rare mineral was on the surface of one of the hottest deserts in the world. Just what was it doing here?

Garvie launched a deep dive into the scientific literature and reconstructed the sequence by which this material came to rest in the desert. As it turns out, saguaros take up calcium—and lots of it—in groundwater. Excess calcium can be toxic so saguaros, like many other plants, safely sequester the mineral in their tissues in the form of insoluble calcium oxalate crystals. After most of the saguaro tissue has rotted away, these oxalate crystals remain as a kind of sand-like material. Even the calcium oxalates, however, don't last forever. In time, a specialized group of bacteria, known as oxalotrophic bacteria, which feed exclusively on oxalate crystals, begin to break them down. The final product? Chunks of monohydrocalcite, like the kind that launched Garvie's inquiry. Over time, the desert heat further transforms these chunks into calcite, a stable mineral that becomes mixed into the local soils.

When it comes to the rare, Soviet-era-sounding minerals that Garvie discovered in the hot rot of saguaro flesh, well, it's unlikely that companies will be filing mining claims any time soon. On the other hand, studying the transformation of calcium oxalate crystals into hydrated calcium carbonate may offer some interesting biomimetic insights. For example, scientists have studied the potential of forests to sop up the excess carbon in the atmosphere that leads to global warming. But these same trees release the stored carbon as carbon dioxide when they decompose. Saguaros and other cactuses, on the other hand, also take up CO_2 during their lifetimes but, as Garvie has shown, after they die, microbial helpers transform the carbon calcium oxalates into a stable, inert minerals that can't easily escape back into the atmosphere. Could mimicking this microbial process suggest another pathway for creating calcium carbonate for use in cement, an energy-intensive building materials? "It started with a scientific curiosity, and it's leading to some interesting research," Garvie says. "We really don't know where this research is going to go. Is it just fun research or is there a bigger story that will come out of it?"

4

TALES FROM THE
BELLY BUTTON

DURING HER FRESHMAN YEAR AT NORTH CAROLINA
State University in 2009, Britné Hackett learned of
a program that offered aspiring research scientists
a spot in a university lab along with professional
training and mentorship. The opportunity seemed
like a perfect fit. "I had always envisioned my-
self in a white lab coat doing medical research,"
Hackett observes.

She applied and landed a post in Professor Rob
Dunn's lab. She was assigned to a team studying
the social transmission of fungal disease in a colo-
ny of North Carolina ants. Little did she know that
the course of her life was about to change—and in
a way she never could have imagined.

It all started the day the newbie scientist
looked up from the lab's ant nest and posed a few

questions to postdoctoral researcher Jiri Hulcr. Hackett's queries were at once beguilingly simple and profound. What exactly was a fungus? she wondered. And what was its function, especially if it sickened and sometimes killed its hosts? One thing led to another and the two soon were discussing the fact that, like ants, human bodies were, well, crawling with microscopic organisms—bacteria, mites, molds, yeasts and fungi, to name a few. "It was amazing to me that there are things that walk around with you on your body that you can't see. I wanted to see them," Hackett says.

So Hulcr and Hackett decided to ask their lab mates to swab their own skin so that they could culture the microbes in Petri dishes. Because belly buttons were likely to be overlooked in the scrubbing of a daily shower, Hulcr's wife, Andrea Lucky, suggested that they might be an especially rich reservoir of microbial biodiversity from which to draw samples. Happy to play along with the lark, the lab's students, along with director Dunn, obliged by dropping their waistbands.

A photograph of each Petri dish, labeled with the name of its donor, appeared on the lab's New Year's card. Hulcr's meager sprinkling of microorganisms fell into the category "Too Much Scrubbing." Dunn's culture, even sparser, was filed in the column "Wimpy Sampling." Hackett's thick impasto of microbial growth was classified, along with two others, as "Healthy Ecosystem." The card was sent not only as a New Year's greeting but also as a celebratory salute to the "diversity of both the microbes as well as us, people."

But after the laughter had died down, the scientists began to take a closer look. A really close look.

What they discovered led them back into evolutionary history as well as catapulted them into the chronic health woes of contemporary society. At the time, the lab's research had begun to move in a new direction. Dunn decided to chart a course to take their inquiries deeper into the waters of public engagement. "One way to make science public," Dunn explained, "is to work with people to study their own lives." What better way to kick off a new citizen science campaign, they reasoned, than to ask participants to do a little navel gazing? And so in 2011, the Belly Button Biodiversity Project (BBBP) was launched.

To date, the BBBP has collected, genetically sequenced and analyzed samples from the belly buttons of more than 583 volunteers around the country. News updates of the results were reported on National Public Radio and in the *New York Times*, *Scientific American*, *Atlantic Monthly* and *Slate*. From the data also has come a scientific paper that was published in a 2012 issue of the journal *PLOS ONE*.

"Belly buttons are ridiculous," Dunn wrote in a September 2013, blog for *Scientific American*, "and yet the life we study in them is not; it includes both dangerous and life-saving species, though in just what mix and why, well, that is what we'd like to know."

•

An estimated 100 trillion microbes live on or in the human body. A fine sheath of teeming life, what Dunn calls our "verdant cloak of existence," lives between our toes and in our eyelashes, under our fingernails and on the soft patch of skin behind our ears. "There are more bacterial cells on you right now than there ever were bison on the Great Plains, more microbial cells, in fact, than human cells," writes Dunn in his 2011 book *The Wildlife of Our Bodies: Predators, Parasites, and Partners That Shape Who We Are Today*.

Collectively, these organisms, invisible to the naked eye, occupy a world that is as wild and biodiverse as any terrestrial or aquatic ecosystem on Earth. This newly discovered realm, known as the human microbiome, is generating a lot of buzz in scientific circles these days, even though it's been right under our noses—quite literally—for eons.

In 2008, the National Institutes of Health launched a five-year initiative, known as the Human Microbiome Project, to learn more about the microorganisms that live in close association with people. The preliminary results have been nothing short of astounding. To date, for example, HMP researchers have counted 75-100 species of bacteria that reside in the human mouth. Based on the current rate of discovery, they estimate that the final tally will exceed 5,000 species. More than 1,000 species of bacteria make their home in the human gut, not to mention scores of fungal species.

The Belly Button Diversity Project only compounds the wonders and mysteries of these NIH findings. The researchers in Dunn's lab turned up 2,300 species in the 500-plus samples they collected. Only a small subset—a mere eight species—appeared frequently (and these were members of families that occur in dry, nutrient-poor conditions, like the "desert that is your body," Dunn quips). Scores of microorganisms were new to science—and not just unidentified species but also whole new genera that remain to be characterized.

Then there were the curious puzzlers. How did a bacterium associated with pesticides, for example, show up in Dunn's sample? And what about the belly button that contained a bacterium whose only other documented location was in a soil sample in Japan? The cause of the riddle? The donor had never set foot in Japan.

For some people, the yuk factor of the microbial cloak is enough to send them screaming into the shower. Increasingly, however, researchers are cautioning against hyper-hygiene practices like the daily rinse. They're discovering that our microbial roomies are essential to human health and well-being. Many of them help ward off pathogens. Human skin cells, for example, exude waxy secretions that feed beneficial bacteria. In exchange, the bacteria emit moisturizing films that soften skin, preventing dry cracks that, like back doors left open, allow ill-intentioned intruders to gain entry into the body. Other bacteria teach skin cells to distinguish allies from mischief makers, enabling the cells to develop their own defensive antibiotics. Six hundred species of bacteria float in human breast milk, inoculating the guts of infants with the microbes they need to absorb vitamins, minerals and calories from the food they eat. Curiously, in this microbial bath scientists also have discovered sugary bribes known as oligosaccharides. The sugars appear to be designed not as nourishment for infants, who are unable to digest them, but as sustenance for a cadre of good gut bacteria that keep bad actors from colonizing a baby's digestive tract.

Increasingly, scientists and health experts now implicate our sterile modern environments—their hypercleanliness, wanton use of antibiotics, their simplification of plant and animal diversity—for the growing incidence of autoimmune and chronic inflammatory disorders including asthma, Crohn's disease and multiple sclerosis, even obesity and diabetes. "If the germ theory is the idea that the presence of bad species can make you sick, the growing sense seems to be that the opposite can also be true. We can get sick because of the absence of good species—or even just the absence of the diversity of species," Dunn writes. These insights have given rise to a healing modality known as medical ecology in which doctors assume a new role as "microbial wildlife managers," writes Carl Zimmer in a 2012 article in the *New York Times*.

•

When it comes to the human microbiome, the surprises, the mysteries and the possibilities seem endless. "The closer you look, the more you find," says Susan M. Huse, a scientific contributor to the microbiome project.

Looking closer at the invisible world around us has become a mantra for Britné Hackett as well. Back when the first belly-button cultures began to grow, she recalls, "I was thinking that all the plates were going to come back with lots of similar-looking white clumps. When I saw all the differences, I thought wow! It opened up this new realm of more and more questions. I started to learn just what research really is all about after that."

These days the hunt for the invisible fuels Hackett's inquiries as a budding young scientist, both in and outside the lab. She credits her early ant work for helping her to become comfortable around insects, allowing her to work on another project in the Dunn lab: the Arthropods of Our Homes. These days her job is to catalogue bugs collected from residences in the Raleigh-Durham area for an exhibition at the North Carolina Museum of Natural Sciences. "We live around these things," Hackett points out. "We're in constant interaction with them, but we just don't pay attention. How many different kinds of ants live in your backyard? You might have one from Japan. You may have an Ethiopian fly just chilling on your windowsill."

"Every day to me is miraculous," she says. "I have this new understanding and appreciation. I want other people to have the same thing."

5

SMALL WORLDS
IN A BIG SPACE

THERE ARE PLACES IN ARCHES NATIONAL PARK where you can stand on the edge of a cliff, gaze out over the Big Empty of the Colorado Plateau and swear with both hands on a bible that nothing, nothing lies between you and eternity. These wide-open spaces, framed by flying buttresses of red rock arches, are so knee-buckling beautiful that they attract visitors from around the world. One is even featured on the Utah state license plate.

On today's visit to the park, though, my eyes are glued not to the horizon but to the ground to keep from twisting an ankle as I pick my way up ledges or drop over slickrock balds. I'm hiking off the beaten track on this hot day in late July with ecologist Tim Graham, scrambling to keep pace with his deliberate, but steady, clip. Now and again, though, I interrupt the rhythm of our crunching boots to lag behind and admire the fluted grain of wind-scoured Navajo sandstone as it flows across canyon walls like long, loosening braids of human hair.

Tim, by contrast, navigates this unmarked terrain with the sure-footedness of someone who could traverse it with his eyes closed. He has spent most of his adult life in and around Moab, Utah, including a stint as a biologist for the U.S. National Park Service in southeastern Utah. He has crisscrossed the Colorado Plateau, from Grand Staircase-Escalante National Monument to the San Rafael Swell, probably about as many times as he's run up and down the ball field in town where he plays pick-up soccer several times a week.

About 45 minutes into our trek, Tim slips off his pack and settles down next to a shallow depression the size of a Thanksgiving turkey platter. It's the first stop on a tour that I have been looking forward to for years. "Time for some belly science," he announces with a smile. I look at Tim, then down at the ground. Although the rock is not quite hot enough to fry an egg, it is, nonetheless, mid-day in mid-summer in the middle of the desert with air temperatures pushing triple digits and not a cloud or speck of shade in sight. But I'm not missing this show for the world. Living here in the dimples of slickrock—weathering pits known as desert potholes—are the tiny descendants of species that have called this wind-scoured place home since the Mesozoic era. To appreciate them, you have to adjust your sights. So I drop to my knees and then gingerly lower my stomach onto the toasty rock.

•

Desert potholes have been on my list of Ten Things to See Before I Die, ever since I had read about them in a guide to canyon country five years ago. Southern Utah is ground zero for potholes. They are so common that the map is, well, riddled with them: Pothole Point in nearby Canyonlands National Park, Swiss Cheese Ridge around Moab and Waterpocket Fold at Capitol Reef National Park, for instance.

My guide doesn't get any more expert than Tim, who has studied these diminutive ecosystems since 1987. He even has the discovery of a new species to his credit—a yet-unnamed oribatid mite that lives only in pools on the Colorado Plateau. Just one other species within this new genus has been identified, and it lives clear across the country in the granite domes of Georgia. Another very similar mite, in the genus *Aquanothrus*, is found in ephemeral pools in South Africa.

Potholes, like the shallow depression we're looking at, typically begin to form when precipitation collects in low points along fractures in the sandstone. Studies by Jim Davis of the Utah Geological Survey and his colleagues reveal that the sandstones are composed almost entirely of grains of silica with only small amounts of calcium carbonate and iron binding them together. Over time, the standing rainwater in these self-contained pools can dissolve this weak cement and liberate the sand grains, as can the mechanical action of freezing and thawing. Strong winds carry off the loose sediments, in essence excavating the pits like a slow-motion backhoe. Natural forces acting on vastly different time and spatial scales produce potholes that range from hollows the size of a teacup to ephemeral ponds that are some 50 feet deep.

Tim pokes around the thin, powdery layer of sand that has collected at the bottom of the pothole. It looks dry and lifeless. A black bathtub ring of live, but desiccated, microorganisms around its rim however, indicates that it contained rainwater at some point during the year. This community, which includes several species of bacteria, forms an impermeable biofilm that keeps the water from seeping through the sandstone. And where there's a sign of water in a pothole, there's a good chance of finding other kinds of life too. Tim carefully isolates a few dark particles that look, to my untutored eye, like tiny flakes of cracked black pepper. They are oribatid mites.

Tim pulls out his water bottle, pours a few tablespoons of liquid over them and then pauses to deliver a brief introduction to mite ecology. Most oribatids are terrestrial and live on plants or in duff on the forest floor where they consume fungi and organic detritus. The three pool-dwelling species of mites, on the other hand, have adapted to life in water. And unlike their vegetarian cousins on land, these mites are omnivores, supplementing a diet of algae and detritus with invertebrates such as nematodes and tiny hunter-orange animals known as rotifers.

Tim pauses in his lesson and trains a magnifying lens on the mites. In this short time, they have been roused from their torpor and have begun kicking around on the edge of the dirt. Their movements are labored and unsteady because mites have pointy, sickle-shaped structures at the end of their feet. In terrestrial environments, they serve as grappling hooks for hanging on to plant material. Even though the appendages are ill-adapted for life in aquatic environments, the pool-dwelling mites have retained these features. The mites are especially ungainly when trying to maneuver through long strands of slick algae, a little like walking in high heels through a bathtub of spaghetti. "They're not very graceful," Tim points out. "They're falling all over each other. They get tangled up."

Tim had observed this behavior early in his pothole studies and confronted a puzzling question. How did the mites survive, he wondered, when one of their staple prey—rotifers—slip in and out of the pores between sand grains with extraordinary ease? These rotifer movements, he says, "are very much like a ballet. How do these clumsy guys feed on these very coordinated, elegant rotifers?"

The answer, it turns out, seems to lie in their differential responses to drought. Every member of a pothole community possesses some extraordinary adaptation for surviving the vagaries of desert rainfall, which is scarce and unpredictable. Even when it does rain, many pools evaporate quickly in the desert's dry air. In this sense, growth and reproduction in desert potholes are a lot like life on the battlefield—long periods of down time during dry intervals punctuated by spurts of frantic energy during wet ones.

Pothole animals ride out the wild surf of boom-and-bust uncertainty by using one of three survival strategies. The drought escapers include vertebrates such as red-spotted toads and winged insects such as backswimmers and mosquitoes. They possess fast-whirring biological clocks that allow young tadpoles and larvae to quickly mature into adulthood and leave the pool before it dries up.

The drought tolerators stay put and endure punishing conditions that would kill most other animals. Through a process known as cryptobiosis, tiny organisms such as tardigrades and rotifers, as well as the eggs of a trio of freshwater crustaceans—fairy shrimp, tadpole shrimp and clam shrimp—can lose up to 95 percent of their total body water. The eggs can survive 50 years or more on a lab shelf. So tough are they in this cryptobiotic state that astronauts have taken them out of the shelter of space capsules and exposed them to the vacuum of outer space and the full ionizing radiation of the Sun with no deleterious effects. Biomimicry enthusiasts know these organisms as the biological models for creating long-lived vaccines that can be stored without refrigeration.

Other pothole dwellers utilize a third approach, what Tim calls the "Tupperware strategy." Snails retreat into their shells and close their openings using a structure known as the operculum, which means "little lid." The mighty mites produce sealants such as waxy cuticles and burrow into the mud to minimize water loss.

Each strategy has its trade-offs. Because they are able to retain a large percentage of their body moisture, mites can spring to life as soon as moisture frees them from their dry matrix of soil. Without water, however, the mites can't survive much longer than a year. The desiccated rotifers, on the other hand, can persist for longer periods in their cryptobiotic state. The downside, though, is that it can take anywhere from five to ten minutes to rev up their metabolic motors once rain falls. The mites are able to exploit this lag time, teetering across the sand on their tippy, high-heeled feet as they feast on the comatose rotifers.

After nearly an hour beside the dried pool, it is time to leave. We have several other potholes to visit before the day is over. By the time Tim has packed up his water bottle and magnifying glass, the sediment already has begun to dry and once again encase the mites in their sarcophagi of silica. I rise slowly to my knees and lean over to peer one last time into the pit. Ecologists call this a Mesozoic lifeboat niche. Hundreds of millions of years ago, the species they now shelter were more widespread. But aquatic predators, including fish and diving beetles, largely eliminated them from the more hospitable habitats of permanent water. So, pothole organisms hedged their bets and evolved over time to make the best of a tough situation. And tough it is. Time and again before the year is out, the tiny mites and their neighbors will endure wild swings in temperature, salinity, pH, and oxygen and carbon dioxide concentrations as their little pool refills and then dries out again.

I read recently that the universal posture of awe and reverence across the world is to bow, kneel or prostrate oneself. The fact that I am ending my first visit to a pothole on my knees seems a fitting response to the wonder of the occasion.

6

IT'S THE MIX NOT THE
MATCH THAT MAKES
THE MAGNIFICENT MOLE

WHEN I WAS A KID, MY FRIENDS AND I SPENT MANY hours tinkering with a toy called Mr. Potato Head. A shapeless, plastic spud, Mr. Potato Head could be accessorized with an assortment of goofy features: bug eyes and jug ears, mustachioed schnozzes, gangly legs attached to clodhopper shoes. No technical skill was required; just the willingness to suspend one's sense of propriety and proportion. Indeed, courting outrageousness was key to the enjoyment of the game.

Judging by the kinds of photographs that appear on our wall calendars, screensavers and Flickr accounts, you might assume that nature never took this bric-à-brac approach to design. We are drawn to images that showcase nature's symmetry, elegance and restraint like the delicate radials of a spider web or the Fibonacci whorls of neatly packed seedheads or the patterned panes of color on a butterfly's wing. It's as if nature were always decked out for opening night at the opera and never for a masquerade ball. Yet nature courts outrageousness more often than we think, takes tongue to cheek, jabs thumb to eye and wreaks more than a little Mr. Potato Head havoc with its designs. Witness the male fiddler crab which grows one claw far larger than the rest. Sidling along marsh flats, he holds this exaggerated appendage slightly aloft and crooked like a man with a bandaged arm about to elbow his way into a crowded bar. Behold too the moose whose rectangular bulk, like a massive sideboard, perches on improbably tall legs. Recall its long-faced homeliness and the furred bell slung under its chin, features that give the animal an uncanny resemblance to Abe Lincoln.

When it comes to winning the grand prize for ungainly proportions and strange add-ons, however, (what science writer Natalie Angier calls the "all-star uglies"), few animals can best the star-nosed mole. This palm-sized mammal inhabits wetlands from southeastern Canada into the eastern U.S. Although it sports a lustrous coat of dark, mink-like fur, the haute couture ends there. In true Mr. Potato Head fashion, star-nosed moles are endowed with squints of bead-black eyes and outsized front paws that are as scaly as chicken feet. Shaped like catcher's mitts, each paw ends in a set of curved, pearly-pink nails that are as long as they are tough. Then there's the matter of the animal's tail. Highly irregular in its thickness, it constricts at the base, swells along the midsection and tapers at the end like a snake that's gorged on a nest of day-old mice.

Nothing, however, can top the animal's nose. Sprouting from its snout is a circlet of 22 fleshy appendages that are so nimble and mobile that they seem to have a life of their own. This pink, anemone-like organ elicits unequivocal disgust. "Like fresh bits of sirloin being extruded through a meat grinder," cried Angier in a 2010 *New York Times* article entitled "Masterpiece of Nature? Yuck!" "Petals on a nightmarish flower," wrote Carl Zimmer in *Discover* magazine. "A Medusa-like rosette," exclaimed mole experts Martyn Gorman and R. David Stone.

All joking aside, the judgments we make about star-nosed moles and other organisms, what we consider yucky or pleasing, funny or scary, soothing or appalling, carry serious implications. They often seal the fate of many of the creatures around us. Witness the 2007 report from a trio of wildlife biologists who placed lifelike rubber replicas of turtles and snakes in the middle of a roadway along the Canadian shore of Lake Erie and stood back to record what happened. Of the 2,000 drivers studied, 2.7 percent went out of their way to intentionally squash the decoys. Reptiles aren't the only animals to be persecuted. In some parts of the country, drivers routinely swerve to flatten armadillos, opossums, slugs or such road-kill feeders as ravens and vultures.

Aesthetic judgments even appear to bias scientists, the very people who might help to rehabilitate the reputations of so-called ugly organisms by bringing to light the elegant ways in which they execute complex tasks or the beneficial roles they play in keeping ecosystems whole and healthy. Alas, it turns out that scientists can get suckered in by a pretty face as much as the rest of us. In a 2010 study in *Conservation Biology*, biologists Morgan J. Trimble and Rudi J. Van Aarde of the University of Pretoria in South Africa reviewed the scientific literature for about 2,000 animal species in South Africa. Their conclusion: a few species hogged the lion's share of scientific resources and attention whereas information for many other species was "virtually nonexistent." The average number of scientific publications for threatened species of large mammals, for example, was more than 500 times that of threatened amphibians. "In the eyes of science," the authors observe, "all species are not created equal."

Why the disparity? Scientists, it turns out, likely harbor many of the same biases as the general public. Commonly studied species, Trimble and Van Aarde write, also tend to be the most charismatic. "Most scientists are in it for the love of what they do," Trimble reported to Angier in the *New York Times*, "and a lot of them are interested in big, furry cute things."

•

This explains why I've been such a diehard fan of the work of Dr. Ken Catania ever since reading about his research on star-nosed moles in the 1990s. As the story goes, Catania was "star-struck" as a young graduate student in neurobiology at the University of California, San Diego. In a 2008 article in *SEED* magazine, neuroscientist Glenn Northcutt, Catania's graduate advisor, recalls that his student was adamant about studying the obscure mammal, even going so far as to declare to Northcutt, "I want to work with star-nosed moles, and if you don't let me, I'm going to go to another lab."

Catania didn't focus on star-nosed moles because they were the easiest, most direct route to a Ph.D. True, the animals only grow up to seven inches long and weigh in at an average of two ounces; yet studying them in the wild is fraught with challenges. Although the animals are wide-ranging, they spend most of their lives underground, using their massive front paws like powerful shovels to excavate tunnels through mucky wetland soils, working at remarkable speed. Scientists observed one mole, for example, that tunneled 235 feet in a single night. Many burrows open up into streams and ponds where the moles' broad, flat paws become amphibious-assault gear, propelling them through the water to intercept aquatic staples such as crayfish, insects and even frogs and fish.

Carrying out research on moles in captivity isn't easy either. As laboratory subjects go, moles are fairly high-maintenance animals. They require large containers of soil and have voracious appetites, consuming their weight in worms daily.

Catania is an example of what can happen when a scientist plies his trade of patient observation and is fearless about beating the bush in pursuit of his curiosity, wherever it might lead him. In the process, he has slowly nudged the needle of public opinion from repugnance to respect when it comes to his odd little subjects, including their chopped-sirloin noses, which Catania's research has shown is not related to their sense of smell. So why then do they go to such great lengths where their sniffers are concerned?

Microscopic analysis of the nose surface has revealed a honeycomb pattern of tightly packed pimple-like structures, known as papillae. Named Eimer's organs in honor of the German scientist Theodor Eimer, who in 1871 discovered similar features on the plain noses of European moles, each papilla contains a core of epidermal cells that function as sensory receptors. Although it measures only about 0.6 inches from tip to tip at its widest point, the nasal structure of star-nosed moles contains more than 25,000 Eimer's organs.

Some scientists initially suggested that the animal's nasal frill is used to detect the electrical fields created by the sweat and mucous of its prey. Catania, on the other hand, demonstrated that the Eimer's organs do something altogether different. An examination of the mole's brain showed that a larger-than-average portion of the cortex was devoted to somatosensory processing; that is, making sense of the blitz of stimuli relayed by the sense of touch. Some of that information was coming from the mole's tail. When held erect, it trails along the ceiling of the mole's underground tunnels, much the way human hands might feel their way down a dark corridor. The tail performs a double duty. During winter, it also stores fat like a portable pantry. When prey becomes scarce, the mole simply draws on these reserves to tide it over to better times.

The majority of the somatosensory information, however, is gathered by the mole's nasal appendage. From there, it travels to the animal's brain on a neural highway made up of more than one hundred thousand nerve fibers. This is nearly six times the number of neural connections between the human brain and hand. According to a paper published by Catania and fellow neuroscientist Jon Kaas, the mole's nose "is clearly a major source of information about the mole's external environment and may be one of the most sensitive and highly developed touch organs among mammals."

This combination of somatosensory hardware and software allows the animal to receive an extremely refined tactile impression of everything it encounters. When searching out prey, for example, the tentacles are extended in a forward position, "fingering" the surrounding world. When the mole lifts its nose, the tentacles retract. So swift is this back-and-forth motion, that at every second the tentacles touch a different area—not once but ten times or more. With response times measured in nano increments, the moles are able to distinguish a worm from a tree root and snap it up faster than a hungry youngster can slurp a spaghetti noodle.

By analyzing cross-sections of brain tissue, Catania made one of the most astounding discoveries of all: the star pattern of the nasal tentacles is mirrored in the actual structural pattern of the brain.

These are just some of Catania's amazing neuroscience discoveries. Along the way, however, he has pursued some quirky sidelines, spinning the straw of ordinary observation into the gold of scientific discovery. Catania is the first scientist to capture pregnant moles from the wild and to observe the birth and development of their young.

In newborn moles, the star-shaped appendages appear as embedded ridges on the face, giving the animals a kind of wrinkled muzzle. In week-old moles, the epidermal tissue that encases the stars sloughs off, revealing the more defined contours of the tentacles. Shortly thereafter, the appendages detach from the face and assume the free radial form of the adult mole. It turns out that this is a unique pathway for appendage development in animals which, typically, be they fingers on a monkey, antennae on a moth or wings on a bird, are all outgrowths of a body wall. Not so the mole's nasal frill.

That's not all. Catania noticed that when the animals swim underwater, they blew bubbles—lots of them. In 2006, he published research in the journal *Nature* showing that star-nosed moles and a species of water shrew (*Sorex palustris*) can smell their prey while submerged. They do so by rapidly exhaling and inhaling bubbles, between five and ten times per second. The exhaled bubbles pick up odor molecules. When inhaled, these molecules alert the animals to the presence of prey. The moles and water shrew became the first mammals discovered to use underwater olfaction, an ability that earned them a place in the zoological history books.

As if this research were not quirky enough, Catania also investigated the field methods of the commercial earthworm pickers in Appalachia who supply his lab moles with food. Using a time-honored tradition known as worm grunting, the harvesters create underground vibrations by drawing a metal rod against a wooden stake in the ground. The action routs earthworms out onto the forest floor by the thousands. Explanations of this phenomenon abound, including one by Charles Darwin in his famous 1881 treatise on earthworms. He suggested that beating the ground created vibrations that were similar to those made by burrowing moles. Earthworms fled to the surface, he conjectured, where their mole predators would not follow them. In a 2008 article in *PLoS One*, Catania affirmed Darwin's hypothesis, demonstrating that worm grunters mimicked the sounds of approaching moles.

From time to time, I check in with Catania's lab to see what surprising new insights he and his grad students are generating. I find this work to be a source of hope and good cheer. Maybe it has something to do with the MacArthur Fellowship, the so-called genius grant, that Catania won in 2006. In a roundabout way, it affirms for me that there is still something a little right about a world that would confer one of its most prestigious awards on someone doing this kind of work.

Asked in 2006 what he planned to do with his MacArthur money—$500,000 of no-strings-attached funding—Catania replied, "I'll continue to examine the most interesting species not in the mainstream—the sort of animals that tell us a lot about brains and how they work," including how our human brains work. Therein lies perhaps the most important finding of all: that ugliness, like beauty, is only skin deep and that if we're willing to dig, even just a little, we'll find enough mystery and amazement in the world around us to occupy us for a lifetime.

7

THE UTILITY OF AWE

"The more we learn about the mystery, the more we will admire it. Mystery and magic never really go away."

From *Survival of the Beautiful* by
David Rothenberg

EARLY ONE MORNING THIS PAST SUMMER I WOKE TO the eastern horizon banked high with blue-gray clouds. They doused everything with a dull ashen light, draining colors and flattening textures so that the desert mountain behind my house took on the pewter tones of a landscape photograph from the 19th century. I pulled a camp chair down into a low point in the garden where I usually sip my first cup of coffee among totems of saguaro cactus and the wild-flung stems of creosote bush.

The day opened soft and cool, more like Seattle than blistering Phoenix. Just as I leaned back to savor the unexpected reprieve from the heat, the sun slowly began to clear the cloud wall behind me. As if on a dimmer switch, the light brightened by degrees, a glow spreading to the crowns of the cactus and then widening until it spotlighted the ridges a quarter-mile distant. Many plants in the desert reflect sunlight as a way of dodging the intensity of its focus. They bristle with translucent spines. Some encapsulate seeds in miniature balls of plush white hairs. Others buff their surfaces with a layer of wax or resin. The strike of light on each needle, each leaf, each pod can sometimes cause the place to spangle, as if the plants were hung with chips of polished glass. I was stunned. I had expected an ordinary day, a routine cup of morning coffee. Instead, I suddenly found myself far from a familiar shore, swimming in a spilled cargo of winking stars.

This is awe and wonder, to be caught unawares by something big, like beauty, that sneaks up from behind, cups your elbow and steers you into a place you hadn't expected to go. "Wonder is anything taken for granted...suddenly filling with mystery," writes David James Duncan in his book *My Story as Told by Water*. "Wonder is anything closed, suddenly opening."

•

Academic psychologists know relatively little about awe—and even less about the things that provoke it, like beauty. Until recently, most studies have focused on the six classic emotions: anger, disgust, fear, sadness, happiness and surprise. I was astonished to learn that "the field of emotion research is almost silent with respect to awe," despite the fact that "awe is central to the experience of religion, politics, nature, and art. Fleeting and rare, experiences of awe can change the course of a life in profound and permanent ways," write psychologists Dacher Keltner of the University of California, Berkeley, and his colleague Jonathan Haidt of the University of Virginia in a pioneering 2003 paper.

The reasons for this oversight are complicated. I suspect that "serious" researchers have avoided the subject because awe often is perceived as a kind of emotional inebriation, a little sloppy, soft-headed and embarrassing like the sentimental uncle who launches into a tipsy riff each year at the Thanksgiving table.

But there are other, more practical reasons why the subject of awe has escaped scholarly notice. Studying it is challenging on many fronts. As far as we know, animals don't experience awe, so researchers cannot learn from analogues in the lab. Moreover, the experience of awe relies on two essential triggers: serendipity and a scope of confounding size. Awe's episodic, ephemeral nature makes it difficult to conjure on the spot. Keltner describes it as a "Zen-like challenge": an attempt to measure something "which might transcend measurement, planning what can only be unexpected, capturing what is beyond description." Awe, he explains, is an encounter with something far larger than the customary confines of the self or one's ordinary frame of reference. It "requires vast objects—vistas, encounters with famous people, charismatic leaders, 1,000-foot-tall skyscrapers, cathedrals, supernatural events—that don't fit well in the fluorescent-lighted 9"×12" space of a lab room."

The results of ingenious new research suggests that the experience of awe not only has the potential for personal transformation but also may be critical to societal well-being. It may even have played an evolutionary role in the survival of our species. The emotion promotes a lessening of what Keltner calls "the press of self-interest." In one early experiment, Keltner and his colleague Lani Shiota asked participants to recall a peak experience while out in nature such as listening to the breaking waves of the Pacific Ocean or walking through the dappled light of a forest of big trees. Study subjects commonly experienced feelings of diminishment, relaying such observations as "I felt small or insignificant." They also became less preoccupied with the self, volunteering such comments as "I was unaware of my day-to-day concerns." At the same time, they registered a sense of expansiveness and connection. "I felt the presence of something greater than myself," some reported or "I felt connected with the world around me."

Subsequent research, such as a 2012 study by a trio of researchers from Stanford University and the University of Minnesota, supports the finding that the experience of awe makes us less self-absorbed and more social, more open to connection. Some of the study's participants, for example, were exposed to awe-eliciting video clips or asked to read or write about experiences of awe. Those who viewed snippets of encounters with whales or massive waterfalls reported responses that were dramatically different from, say, those who simply watched footage of happy people waving flags through a rain of confetti at a city parade. In follow-up surveys of the two groups, the awe-exposed participants felt as if they had more time, were less impatient, were more willing to volunteer to help other people, valued experiences more than material goods and reported a bigger bump in life satisfaction.

From these and other studies, Keltner and his colleagues conclude that awe has the capacity for creating greater openness, generosity, a willingness to connect, to help others, to collaborate. Writer Duncan summed up the positive influence of awe on human behavior like this: "I believe some people live in a state of constant wonder," he declared. "I believe they're the best people on Earth."

•

On late Saturday afternoons in mid-winter, I like to hike into the interior of a desert mountain behind my house to a place called Pima Canyon. One south-facing slope hosts a particularly fine example of what's known as a devil's garden. These places are so-named for the spiny cholla cactus that tend to congregate in dense stands. Chollas are infamous for their sausage-shaped joints that can be easily dislodged from the plant but not from the fingers or ankles of hikers who become impaled when accidentally brushing up against them. Dead joints the color of dark chocolate adhere along the length of their stalks which can grow to five feet tall. Live plant parts sprout in bristled masses from the crowns of the cactus like matted braids of bleached-blond dreadlocks. In his book *When the Rains Come*, the biologist and desert writer John Alcock observes that the thatch of spines that covers each plant joint is so good at reflecting sunlight that the outer skins of chollas heat up to only fourteen degrees F above ambient air temperatures in the desert's searing heat whereas the cuticles of less spiny cactus can soar to forty degrees F. In laboratory tests, scientists made an even more startling discovery: when they slowly turned up the heat, cholla cactus made biochemical adjustments that enabled them to survive 138 degrees F.

I love these elite thermal athletes, but not just for their extraordinary capacities. In winter the low angle of the setting sun runs through the devil's garden like a wildfire, illuminating each blond spine until the whole hillside glows. Someday, I would like to take a couple neuroscientists into the field, have them string up my head with electrodes and watch their monitor burst into flame when the sunset takes a match to the hillside—and to my heart. "Happens every time," I'll tell them. This is your brain on awe.

For those of us who study and practice biomimicry, awe is regarded as a fringe benefit, albeit a much-valued pleasure. New insights from the academic literature in psychology, however, might offer another, far more serious perspective. I'll wager that the experience of awe drew us to the discipline of biomimicry in the first place. Each one of us could likely point to our own treasured organisms that, like the cholla cactus, inspire with their ingenuity and seduce with their beauty, organisms that we visit time and again in the wild to restore a sense of magnificence to our lives.

I might go one step further, however, to say that the experience of awe not only makes us revisit nature time and again but that it also helps us persist in our search for the secrets to survival and puts us in a frame of mind to make the most of what we find. Positive emotions such as awe actually create the conditions conducive to innovation. I believe this for the reasons that Keltner and his colleagues have proposed: that awe has the capacity for creating greater openness, generosity, a willingness to connect, to help others, to collaborate.

Biomimicry is labor in the trade of wonder. For me, the paycheck is to stand in the midst of an extended family of cholla cactus and feel a throb of gratitude as they ignite with the sunset, burn and then rise again from the ashes of a long winter's night. What astounds even more is this: that at any point in time, we could have taken a wrong exit into a dead end on the long highway of evolution. And yet here we are together in the world, lit with joy and sunlight on an ordinary afternoon in winter. It could have been otherwise—but it wasn't.

"Believe in what lasts," writes David Rothenberg in the *Survival of the Beautiful*, "knowing that evolution has kept these beautiful forms alive because they started out being possible and ended up being actual—not because they had to be, but because they ended up surviving through a mix of randomness and opportunity that likely would not be repeated if we were to roll time back a few million years and start again. So is there nothing especially good about what life strategies and results we have got? They are important because they are there. And we are there too."

8

EARLY WARNING

IN HIS 1982 TRAVEL BOOK *BLUE HIGHWAYS*, WILLIAM
Least Heat Moon included an entry about a visit to
Cave Creek, a stream that flows through a can-
yon on the eastern flanks of the Chiricahuas. To
get to these remote mountains in the far south-
eastern corner of Arizona, the author described
how he drove across the "flat, hot scarcity" of
the Chihuahuan Desert, until he encountered a
stockade of vertical rock columns with no obvious
passageway in sight. Baffled, Least Heat Moon
motored on when suddenly the road seemed to
slip through the façade. Sun-shot desert scrub
gave way to a gallery forest of alligator juniper,
sycamore and white oaks. Threading through the
shade of the trees was a flowing stream, some-
thing that even seasoned desert dwellers might
regard as nothing short of improbable here;
miraculous even. From time to time the canopy

opened to reveal ruddy pinnacles encrusted with yellow and green lichen. Pitted and shaved by the elements over eons, the towering outcrops, he said, "might have come from the mind of Antonio Gaudi."

"How could this place be?" he asked himself, enchanted.

This is the question that occurs to me over and over again as I accompany two graduate students from Oregon State University into Cave Creek Canyon one early morning in June. Our route retraces the first leg of Least Heat Moon's journey, leaving the desert valley to pass through the hoodoo sentinels that stand guard at the canyon entrance. As we gain elevation into forests of Apache and ponderosa pine, we veer from the main road to detour to our destination: a tiny tributary known as Turkey Creek.

We park the car in a small turnout, grab plastic buckets and small hand nets, and follow a trail through a forest so dry that it crunches underfoot. It will be another month before the summer monsoon begins, when enough moisture will well up from the Pacific Ocean and Gulf of California to fuel the muscled thunderheads that pummel this landscape with hard, violent rains. I am surprised, then, when I hear the splash of running water as we draw nearer to the creek. Unlike Cave Creek, which is considered an intermittent stream, Turkey Creek hosts a perennial flow, even though it may shrink during droughty times of the year. At that time it can become little more than a series of stepped pools that are connected by a thin trickle of water; like pearls on a string. Today, however, we settle around a large pool, about the size of a six-person Jacuzzi, which is fed by a gentle water-fall of clear, cool water. Nodding from the stream banks are the delicate spurs of yellow columbine blooms. Somewhere a hermit thrush sounds its call from the forest, a song that is halting, discontinuous and slightly off-key, like an atonal score for clarinet. With it, riding on a downstream breeze, comes the fresh smell of sweet water. I inhale deeply.

This is a mountain in the Chihuahuan Desert. The *desert*, I remind myself. *How could this place be?*

It turns out that this is just the beginning of the day's wonders. We are here to collect the top predator of these tiny streams: *Abedus herberti*, a giant water bug. Student Kate Boersma is exploring how the presence or absence of these bugs can structure the community of organisms that live in these streams and, in turn, regulate some of their basic conditions such as the growth of algae. The "borrowed" bugs will be temporarily put to work in controlled experiments on the grounds of the Southwestern Research Station a few miles down the road.

To simulate the environments in which *A. herberti* live, Boersma has filled a series of plastic tubs with creek water and seeded them with a suite of organisms typically found in Chiricahua waters. Giant water bugs are released into only some of the artificial pools so she can better understand changes in the food web when *A. herberti* is the dominant predator or when, in the absence of the bug, secondary predators such as dragonfly larvae and diving beetles take over. Boersma uses a Sharpie to carefully mark each water bug so that she can return them to their natal waters at the end of her experiment.

Deb Finn, a fellow graduate student in Boersma's lab at OSU, has volunteered to help us harvest bugs from the stream. An experienced bug nabber, Finn wades in first, heading for the deepest parts of the pool. She slowly slides her hand along the undersides of submerged boulders. This is prime real estate for *A. herberti* and where the biggest adults, which grow to about 1.5 inches, can be found clinging to the rocks. I am far more squeamish. If provoked, the bug can sink a beaklike instrument, known as a rostrum, into human flesh. The rostrum serves as a syringe for injecting digestive enzymes into the tissues of their prey and then doubles as a straw for slurping the liquefied remains. Experts maintain that the bite is no worse than a bee sting but I'm not taking any chances. Surely, they haven't earned the nickname "toe-biter" for nothing! So I head for the shallows where I begin to gingerly turn over smaller, palm-sized cobbles and scoop the fleeing bugs with an aquarium net.

Finn is undaunted. Within minutes, she captures a trophy-sized bug and sloshes over to the stream bank to place it gently into one of the buckets. I bend down to get a closer view and yelp with surprise. The bug bristles with club-shaped eggs. A female has laid them end to end in tidy cornrows on the flattened shield of the male's back, one of a series of egg clutches that he is likely to brood that year. Shaped like a high-clearance Hummer that is perched on segmented stilts, the male will stay close to the water's edge, performing slow push-ups that bathe the eggs with oxygen-rich water.

This paternal care of offspring, though common in giant water bugs, is rare among insects.

Although this behavior has earned *A. herberti* marquee billing in the annals of entomology, it isn't the insect's only extraordinary adaptation. David Lytle, an associate professor of zoology at OSU and faculty advisor for Boersma and Finn, recalls one of his discoveries. Standing on the banks of Turkey Creek as a monsoon storm suddenly appeared overhead, Lytle observed how the wingless water bugs, unlike their fellow aquatic organisms, were able to avoid being washed away by the resultant flash flood. While he and his student team scrambled out of the active stream channel to higher ground, dozens of giant water bugs were doing exactly the same thing.

Suspecting that the physical process of falling rain was the trigger for this flight-to-safety behavior (and not changes in barometric pressure or ion concentrations in the stream), Lytle and his student researchers returned on a sunny day, this time packing in a fire hose to spray pools containing *A. herberti* with water. Surprisingly, the responses from the bugs to the simulated rainfall varied stream by stream. Those in watercourses that were rarely flooded were slow to respond to the artificial cues. Some never even budged from the stream channel despite a continuous flow of water from the hose. Those in streams that were often scoured by floodwaters, on the other hand, began their evacuation after only about 20 minutes of simulated rainfall. "It seemed that over hundreds or even thousands of years, evolution had fine-tuned these isolated populations so that their behaviors suited the flood regime of individual streams," observes Lytle in the 2011 book *Wading for Bugs: Exploring Streams with the Experts*.

Could the mechanisms of this flood-detection system in giant water bugs be emulated in early warning devices for humans? Among those to benefit from such a system would be backcountry recreationalists who frequent remote landscapes that are subject to flash floods. In many desert canyons in the Southwest, for example, a blue sky overhead provides unsuspecting hikers no clues that a heavy rainstorm further upstream is sending a roaring wall of water, boulders and tree limbs directly toward them.

The researchers have not determined the mechanism by which the giant water bugs sense the changes in their environment. Vibrations created by powerful monsoon downpours, for example, are known to rouse desert frogs and toads from their underground torpor. Are water bugs responding similarly or is it the sound of raindrops that elicits flood-escape behavior? The interest in potential human applications doesn't end there. Other aspects of the bug's life history could prove useful as well, including mimicking the chemical constituents of the underwater adhesives that females use to glue their eggs to the backs of the males.

Sadly, it is unclear whether giant water bugs in the Chiricahuas will be around long enough for teams of biologists and engineers to pursue these investigations. Genetic research has shown that populations of *A. herberti* have persisted in the perennial streams of the Chiricahuas since the end of the Pleistocene, about 10,000 years ago. Despite this long residency, the research by Boersma and her fellow doctoral students in Lytle's lab, suggests that giant water bugs now face uncertain prospects here. Many climate change researchers predict that the Southwest will become drier in the future. The perennial waters that giant water bugs rely on could disappear in the Chiricahuas, as they already have in the neighboring Whetstone Mountains, where fellow student Michael Bogan has documented localized extinctions of *A. herberti*.

Despite the clear threat, piquing interest in these organisms among natural resource agencies, much less the general public, can be a hard sell. Water bugs, as well as the other stream organisms they prey on, aren't considered pests of timber or agricultural crops or food for a lucrative fisheries industry or vital to maintaining the quality of drinking water for humans.

Could the very etymology of their name ironically predict their future? "The word 'bug' derives from the Middle English word 'bugge' meaning 'spirit' or 'ghost,'" Lytle observes, "and was originally associated with the bed bugs that disappeared in the morning after biting their human victims during the night." Could these extraordinary organisms become the ghosts of desert streams, vanishing long before we discover the miracles of their ordinary lives?

9

THINKING LIKE
AN AGAVE

5:40 A.M. I CATCH THE TAIL END OF THE DAY'S
weather forecast on the radio. The temperature is
already pushing 90 degrees. My heart sinks. June
is living up to its reputation as the hottest month
of the year. For the past week Arizona has been
in the grip of a heat wave, with the thermometer
climbing past 115 nearly every day in the City of
Phoenix where I live. It looks as if today might
break another record.

I throw an extra water bottle into my backpack
as I prepare to head into the field with botanists
from the Desert Botanical Garden (DBG). Although
our destination is Sedona, two hours north and
several thousand feet higher in elevation, tem-
peratures there will still be toasty. To make
matters worse, we'll be hiking out in the open,

bushwhacking to exposed ridges through thickets of spikes where plants go by such names as shindagger, horse crippler and crucifixion thorn. I rifle through a stack of folded trousers on my closet shelf and pick fire-engine-red pants made of a thick, tightly woven cotton, the closest thing I have to Army-issue canvas. I pull them on, look at myself in the mirror and chuckle aloud. Oh well, by the end of the day I may be comatose from heat and exertion but my crimson pants can at least guide the rescue helicopter to my impaled remains in the desert brush.

I meet up with the carpool at Wendy Hodgson's house. All morosity dissipates as I catch sight of Wendy, with an ear-to-ear grin, strolling down the driveway. She calls out her signature greeting, "How ya doin'?" as she grips me in a bear hug. Petite but sinewy, Wendy has lost none of her athleticism since her college days on a golf scholarship. She later earned a graduate degree in botany at Arizona State University in the 1970s. Maintaining physical strength and stamina has been critical to her career since most of her 40-plus years as a DBG researcher have been spent out in the wilds of Arizona.

She has had adventures that leave me bug-eyed and stuttering with envy: rappelling down a Grand Canyon wall to pluck a cliff-edge plant from the Coconino sandstone or shooting the rapids of the Colorado River to collect plants from a remote side canyon. Then there's the time she bivouacked with colleagues in the cinder-cone deserts in the southwestern corner of the state. While pitching their tents, a man walked right out of the horizon and spent the night around their campfire. Their guest turned out to be the famous desert writer Edward Abbey.

Ask Wendy about what tops her list of outdoor adventures, however, and she's most likely to name her longtime love affair with the agaves of Arizona. Great pinwheels of fleshy, spear-like leaves, agaves range widely throughout the state, growing on the desert floor in the shadows of saguaro cactus and all the way up to 8,000 feet in forests dominated by ponderosa pine. To date, researchers have tallied 23 taxa of native agaves, more than half of which are endemic; that is, they occur only in Arizona.

The final tally, however, is far from complete. In the 1930s, when botanists first began to conduct formal field surveys in Arizona, they noted some odd agaves, recording their sightings of these curious anomalies in letters or as hunches on plant lists. Unfortunately, documentation was spotty. The official filing of specimens in herbaria, like the one at the DBG, requires the inclusion of plant parts such as flowers along with leaf samples. Since many agaves bloom during the torrid month of June, when it is torturous, if not dangerous, to be roaming out in the open, the early botanists often encountered these outliers only during the cooler offseason.

In the 1970s, researchers began to suspect that a collection of anomalous agaves near archeological ruins along the Mogollon Rim in north-central Arizona could be remnants of the cultivated gardens of pre-Columbian people. Interest grew and additional plants were discovered. By the late 1980s, two new species of ancient agave cultivars had been named.

Around this time, Wendy too caught agave fever. Then in 1992 she struck gold. While reviewing a plant list for the Grand Canyon in preparation for a collecting trip, she noticed that *Agave parryi*, a native species, was on the list. Wendy knew that the plant had been misidentified since *A. parryi* did not occur in the Grand Canyon. She consulted botanist Art Phillips, her colleague at the Museum of Northern Arizona (MNA), Flagstaff. Art recalled the plant and was able to direct Wendy to its exact location. Sure enough, when she hiked down into the canyon, Wendy found not *A. parryi* but an agave that was unlike any that she had seen before.

As you move north in latitude, agaves typically grow smaller and more compact as a protective response against colder temperatures. This specimen, however, defied the rule. The Grand Canyon agave was large and its leaves widely arrayed. Nearby were some archaeological ruins. Her heart began to pound. "That was my smoking gun," Wendy says. "I knew that it would not have evolved in the Grand Canyon in that form with its big and looser rosettes. It was brought in by people."

After hours of careful comparative analysis with other agaves in the DBG herbarium, Wendy declared the plant a new species and officially christened it *A. phillipsiana* in honor of her MNA colleague. Subsequent genetic tests by fellow DBG botanist Andrew Salywon have confirmed Wendy's designation.

Due mostly to Wendy's field research and Andrew's molecular sleuthing, the tally of domesticated pre-Columbian agaves continues to grow. To date, five species have made the list. The official botanical christening of additional agaves is currently in the works.

As our van finally crunches to a halt on a long dirt road in Sedona's red-rock backcountry, Wendy jumps out and surveys her surroundings. Every outing is a chance to find a new clue in the landscape that can help piece together a picture of a mysterious and fascinating past. To stumble across a new species, especially one that is tied to the lives of ancient people, "is exciting," Wendy says. "It is like YES!"

She raises her arms and begins to shout into the fierce heat of the day. "I love the way this looks, the way it feels, the way it smells. In my next life," she declares, "I want to come back as a field botanist."

•

Sedona is renowned for mesas the color of fresh paprika which rise out of the rolling chaparral of juniper and pinyon pine in the north-central part of the state. I am standing on the top of one of these mesas, looking out over a series of cliff faces, forming what look like basting stitches across the land. At my feet are rows of tumbled rocks, the linear ruins of a prehistoric field house. Eight hundred—maybe even a thousand—years ago, someone took shelter here from the sun or the wind or the rain to keep watch over a hillside planted with agave. The guard would likely have kept a pile of palm-sized stones or a slingshot near at hand to pick off the gophers and packrats foraging for the more tender young plants.

Wendy and Andrew are ecstatic. The two botanists have examined so many agaves up close that even a cursory look at these specimens suggests that they may be candidates for new species status. Many of the agaves are in bloom, which will allow the researchers to bring complete sample sets of leaves and flowers back to the DBG for later analysis. They snap photos and write down the GPS coordinates for each plant. Using long-handled pruning shears, they also snip a blossom from the towering flower stalks. Armed with a sharp knife, Andrew gingerly buries his hands into the rosette to hack off one of its thick leaves, taking care to avoid the serrated teeth along the leaf edge and sharp terminal spine on the end. Ancient pictographs in Mexico show how Mayans inserted these spines into the flesh of children as a form of discipline. Wendy shakes her head at the cruelty of it. On a field outing weeks before, a terminal spine embedded itself in the knuckle of one of her fingers. Measuring almost one centimeter long, the spine caused serious swelling and pain before it had to be surgically removed.

As Wendy and Andrew tend to their plant-collecting regimen, I sit down to examine these plants up close. For ancient people, agaves were one of those all-in-one plants that provided a cornucopia of products. In her book *Food Plants of the Sonoran Desert*, Wendy lists the following benefits of agaves: "food, alcoholic and nonalcoholic beverages, syrup, fiber, cordage, clothing, sandals, nets, blankets, lances, fire hearths, musical instruments, hedgerows (including boundary demarcations), soap, medicine and ceremonial purposes."

In this list of human services, one of the most important was food. During a late stage in their development, agaves flip a metabolic switch and begin to divert huge amounts of energy to the center stem of their rosettes. The plants build this carbohydrate-rich tissue to fuel the growth of a massive flower stalk. Prehistoric people would short-circuit this process by hacking off the rosette of leaves just as the flower stalk formed and began to drain the precious store of nutrients. The size of a basketball, the heart then could be roasted in underground fire pits for several days until it was tender enough to eat.

For prehistoric farmers, agaves must have seemed a kind of miracle food. They grew more labor-intensive crops such as corn, beans and squash in low-lying fields with easier access to irrigation. Agaves, on the other hand, flourished in the thin, rocky soils of the hillsides that overlooked their fields. Aside from the need for pest control of gophers, the plants were fairly self-sufficient. Although agaves reproduce sexually (hence the production of nectar-rich flowers that attract bats, bees beetles and birds), the primary mode of propagation is through cloning. The plants produce genetic copies of themselves via underground rhizomes. Indeed, adult plants at the end of their lifespans are routinely encircled by young clones, known as "pups." Because these young plants are remarkably tough and could survive overland travel in a backpack, they were traded over long distances by people in prehistoric times. Indeed, Wendy suspects that the progenitors for many of the domesticated species of agaves in Arizona came from Mexico. These forgotten species have either become extinct or have yet to be discovered there.

The realization that the plants before me are copies of the very same agaves that prehistoric people tended nearly a millennium before makes me grow flush with wonder and admiration. How have these clones persisted here?

For one thing, their form is well adapted to desert conditions: wide swings in temperature, which can range from triple digits to below freezing, and scant and unpredictable rainfall. Agaves are collecting dishes whose guttered leaves capture this moisture and funnel it to its shallow roots. Plumped-up with rain, the leaves double as storage tanks. At the same time, the rosette pattern protects against water loss as overlapping leaves partially shade each other from the desiccating sun and drying winds in a strategy known as phyllotaxy, in which each leaf spirals off the center at a slightly offset angle in order to balance the need for both sunlight and self-shading. For added measure, a waxy cuticle covers the surface of the leaf, retaining the hard-won moisture.

The plant also draws on a bag of tricks that are invisible to the unaided eye. Its stomata, or "breathing" pores, are recessed, rather than flush with, the leaf's surface. This buffers contact with the dry air that could increase water evaporation during photosynthesis when the stomata are open in the give-and-take of absorbing carbon dioxide and releasing oxygen. During drought periods, some arid-land plants such as agaves practice an alternate method of photosynthesis known as Crassulacean Acid Metabolism (CAM). Stomata open at night, instead of during the day, to minimize water loss. CAM photosynthesis conserves water but dramatically slows plant growth. When moisture is more available and they can afford to forgo greater water loss for faster growth, however, agaves can switch back to opening their stomata during the day.

Then, of course, there is the sheer beauty of these plants: the scallops of fine, regular teeth that run along the edges of their sturdy leaf spears, the attenuated arc of each leaf tip which is every bit as beautiful as the curve in a dancer's wrist as she holds it aloft in space above her head. It is a plant that can flourish in thin soils and sparse rains and yet be of great service and startle with its grace. These are precisely the qualities to which I aspire in my own brief tenure on the planet. I find myself wondering: 1,000 years ago, was there another person here on this very spot, gazing out at the red-rock cliffs who, like me, was astonished and grateful and happy to just quietly sit in the company of these plants?

•

Wendy and Andrew carefully bag and mark each plant sample in paper grocery bags and then gently load them into the back of the van. On the ride back to Phoenix, the van begins to fill with the aroma of agave blossoms: a sweet and musky smell.

It doesn't take long before we cross the frontier of urban sprawl that creeps ever northward from Phoenix to Sedona. As far as the eye can see, a crust of red-tiled roofs is overtaking the desert. In the fall of 2014, this region of Arizona was hit hard by record flooding. Dry washes suddenly raged with floodwaters that jumped their banks and lofted homes off their foundations, pummeling them until they broke into pieces. Cattle and horses swam alongside sofas and empty SUVs.

The desert is adapted to the floods that follow boom-and-bust cycles of rain. Current modes of human development, however, have outstripped the capacity of the land to effectively mitigate storm flows. Instead of designing structures that intercept water onsite, like agaves, saguaro cactus and other desert plants, we armor nearly every surface of our developments, shunting rainfall from roofs, driveways and highways. Hydrologists estimate that these impervious urban surfaces send four times the amount of stormwater across the land than undeveloped desert. Some of these urban flows course into holes in the ground known as retention ponds. More often than not, they are odd, leftover spaces carved out of already anonymous landscaping. Occasionally, these excavations have been integrated into recreational developments, doubling, for example, as ball fields under dry conditions and catchments for stormwater overflow in floods. Yet, in major flood events, even the most thoughtful designs can brim with a murky urban soup which is laced with motor oils, backyard pesticides and the fecal wastes of birds, dogs and cats. Compared with the agave's elegant fit of design to circumstance, our designs often are crude, clumsy and ugly.

What if human-built structures functioned more like agaves, capturing stormwater and discreetly directing it to a storage area where it could service localized needs? What if, in the process, we could marry utility to beauty, which agaves so perfectly model? As an example, I might point to the designs of one of my favorite architects Glenn Murcutt. In his native Australia, water often is as scarce as it is in the deserts of the American Southwest, and so his houses typically incorporate features for rainwater harvesting and storage. The designs for this exterior plumbing, however, are no slam-bam, get-the-job-done affairs.

Take his Magney House in New South Wales. Canted roofs, like the guttered leaves of the agave, funnel rain into a central trough and from there into an underground tank. The rain spout flares in what looks like a receiving bowl or cupped hands. To my eye, it is a beneficent gesture, as if the design were striking a blessing pose, assuming a position of gratitude for the gift of water in dry places.

What if our buildings and roadways, like the Magney House, like the agave, routinely intercepted rainfall onsite before it flowed across the land and conjoined with other flows to form destructive floods? What if they received water as the gift that it is, rather than sloughed it off as a nuisance?

What if our designs, like the agave, could help us flourish in an age of resource scarcity? What if they could be of great service and, at the same time, startle us with their grace?

10

COLLABORATING WITH CHANCE: THE AERONAUTS OF MOUNT ST. HELENS

How do you calculate upon the unforeseen? It seems to be the art of recognizing the role of the unforeseen, of keeping your balance amid surprises, of collaborating with chance, of recognizing that there are some essential mysteries in the world and thereby a limit to calculation, to plan, to control. To calculate upon the unforeseen is perhaps exactly the paradoxical operation that life most requires of us.

From A Field Guide to Getting Lost *by*
Rebecca Solnit

IT IS EARLY NOVEMBER, THE DAY BEFORE THE ROAD to Windy Ridge is scheduled to be closed for the winter. I study the map. The route I will be traveling unspools for 37 miles from the Town of Randle, Washington, climbing some 3,000 feet in elevation through the Cascade Range before dead-ending at Windy Ridge just northeast of Mount St. Helens. My late start means that I will reach the overlook by mid-afternoon. By then the misty rain will have turned to light snow. I look down at my Fiat rental car—a snub-nosed thimble of a vehicle that I had picked out from the Enterprise lot for its gas economy, not horsepower. It is the kind of toy automobile that you might drive into a circus ring for the sole purpose of disgorging an improbable number of fully outfitted clowns before an incredulous audience. En route from the airport in Seattle, however, the Fiat's get-up-and-go surprised me, and so I nicknamed it the Little Italian Stallion. I dismiss my misgivings about its tiny size, turn the key in the ignition and then pat the dashboard. "It's you and me, baby," I say, as I put the car into gear and begin to thread the highway's tight switchbacks.

Even if I were forced to push the balking Stallion up slick mountain grades, I would not miss this journey for anything. I have been fascinated by Mount St. Helens ever since the 1980s when I walked into a friend's living room in Minneapolis and spied a print by landscape photographer Frank Gohlke on her wall. From across the room, the pewter-colored image resembled an abstract expressionist painting: a yin-and-yang composition that featured swirls of what looked like thickly worked paint on one side and a crazy quilt of brushstrokes on the other.

But this was no scene conjured from the imagination. Gohlke shot *Aerial view: shattered logs in south end of Spirit Lake. Four miles north of Mt. St. Helens* from a Cessna while circling the area in 1982, two years after the volcano's dramatic eruption.

The photograph depicted a massive new construction site that was bulldozed and reconfigured by nature when the largest landslide in recorded history roared down Mount St. Helens. The story goes something like this: In the two months leading up to the eruption of Mount St. Helens in May 1980, magma rose beneath the volcano, bumping up against a ceiling of brittle rock on its north face. The pressure eventually created an ominous bulge that grew by as much as five feet per day. Then at 8:32 a.m. on May 18, the bulge suddenly slumped like melting ice cream down the mountain's flank. A series of three landslides gutted the interior of the volcano. Great blocks of rock, trees and earth hurtled down the mountain into the Toutle River Valley which lay to the immediate north of the mountain. In a mere ten minutes, the debris hash stormed through 14 miles of rugged terrain, burying some places to depths of 640 feet.

A part of the avalanche smashed into the south end of Spirit Lake, a much-beloved getaway for generations of vacationers. It was like a sumo wrestler jumping into a bathtub of water, says Todd Cullings, assistant director of the Johnston Ridge Observatory at the Mount St. Helens National Volcanic Monument. The weight of the debris sent a wall of water to the far shore and up a slope that was 850 feet high. As the wave receded, it sucked everything in its path into the lake including forests that had kept watch over Spirit Lake for centuries. When it was all over, so much of the mountain had tumbled into the lake that its floor had been raised by more than 200 feet, causing its surface area to double in size. The pickup sticks in Gohlke's photo were the silvered remains of thousands of massive trees—some of them nearly seven feet in diameter—now floating on their sides and clogging the once deep, blue eye of the alpine lake.

But that was not the end of the story. The mountain would bust a seam and explode sideways, jetting a blast of fractured and pulverized rock and lava. The lateral blast cloud, like a searing, stone-filled wind, raced out of the mountain at velocities of up to 670 miles an hour. Hardest hit was the 30-square-mile Toutle River Valley. Once a verdant basin, it became known as the Pumice Plain after the eruption. Beyond this core, the blast flattened a fan-shaped area of 230 square miles of forests.

On the Pumice Plain, the blast cloud was followed by a series of 18 pyroclastic surges, mixtures of ash, gas and pumice that approached temperatures of 1,500 degrees F. Parts of the plain were so thoroughly cooked that they remained dangerously hot for three years after the eruption. As if for good measure, the volcano doused its handiwork with fragments of rock, lava and ash known as tephra. The north slope alone was buried under several feet of this material which, when moistened by the rain, took on the consistency of wet cement. After a flyover to survey the devastated landscape, then-President Jimmy Carter famously declared: "The moon looks like a golf course compared to this."

What kinds of forces could wreak such devastation? I wondered. I'm certainly not the only one who has found this question intriguing. According to the U.S. Forest Service (USFS), more than half a million tourists visit Mount St. Helens monument each year to stare into the maw of the broken volcano that shed so much earth in the 1980 eruption that it shaved off 1,300 feet from the summit, the equivalent of filling 15 buckets for every man, woman and child on the planet. Like me, they come here to satisfy a yen for what's known as the "apocalyptic sublime"—the desire we seem to have for sipping a disquieting cocktail of beauty, awe and terror while viewing vast landscapes that have been strafed by unfathomable violence.

What's unusual about Mount St. Helens, however, is that the fascination didn't just end with the power of nature's destructive forces. People began to ask: how does life make the transubstantiation from annihilation back into life? It was a beguiling-enough question that the U.S. Congress passed the Mount St. Helens National Volcanic Monument Act in 1982. The legislation created a 110,000-acre national monument for recreation, research and education, a whopping 106,255 acres of which were reserved to allow "geologic forces and ecological succession to continue substantially unimpeded." The law earmarked funding for fundamental field research in geology and ecology within this zone—a provision made all the more remarkable by the fact that it occurred during the science-averse Reagan administration. In the decades that followed, Mount St. Helens would earn the distinction as one of the most exhaustively studied volcanoes on earth.

"Approached attentively," Gohlke writes, "any place may persuade us to linger in an attempt to locate the source of its attraction." Like Gohlke, trapped in his Cessna by the gravitational pull of the mountain's apocalyptic sublime, I set out on my own complicated orbit around this beautiful and difficult place. I started my trek to Windy Ridge in the lowlands at Iron Creek, an old-growth forest of cedar, hemlock and Douglas fir. It was the kind of place that Hollywood might have chosen as the movie set for the retelling of Genesis. Sixty inches of rain fall here annually, 20 inches more than the national average. The precipitation feeds rivulets that tinkle through forest sponge. Both downed and living trees are covered in moss, as if the trunks and branches were wearing pajamas of plush fleece. Everywhere silence swallows sound, except in places like Iron Creek Falls where the stream shoots off a cliff into a crystalline capture pool. The pre-eruption forests around Spirit Lake must have looked something like this: big, big trees, shadows and dim light, moss, silence and the thread of water running through it all like a clear undercurrent of joy.

After gaining some elevation, I stop at Bear Meadow. It was here that camper Gary Rosenquist trained his camera lens on the volcano, manually advancing the film frame by frame at the precise moment when the north flank began to crumple, slipslide and blow up in a series of massive, roiling clouds. The explosion was heard in places as far away as British Columbia and northern California. A strange collusion between topography and the laws of physics, however, created a quiet zone radiating several tens of miles from the epicenter of Mount St. Helens. Not even the residents of Portland, Oregon, at a remove of 50 miles, heard the blast. It is eerie to stand here, knowing that Rosenquist and his fellow campers stood within the quiet zone as they snapped their photos that morning, narrowly missing the blast cloud's searing wind of rock and woody fragments by a mere one-third of a mile. His series of now-famous photographs have allowed geologists to reconstruct the unfolding of the eruption's events. Without them, the precise details of the story that day might have been lost in the clouds of ash and debris.

On this afternoon, mist obscures the peak of Mount St. Helens, whose perfect cone was shattered some 35 years ago. I imagine the mountain as I have seen it in photographs: the half-walls of the crater like a parenthesis embracing a central lava dome. I don't need to see the volcano, however, to gauge how close I am to it. Thirty-five years later the highway is still littered with casualties from the explosions. Tree trunks blackened with rain lie toppled at the side of the road. Others, the color of hoarfrost, are sprinkled across the hillsides, slowly decaying in the very places where they were felled. Bristled clumps of silver fir sprout in patches on the bald ground. From afar, the slopes resemble the coat of a dog with a nasty case of mange.

By the time I get to the Windy Ridge overlook, the temperature has dropped and the clouds are lowering. I hurry up a steep hill, my boots crunching on the putty-colored pumice, nylon poncho snapping in the wind and sleet. I look down on Spirit Lake playing hide and seek in the mist. The scene clears for a few moments and reveals the logjam of trees filling one of its big bays. The lakeshore once sheltered cabins, scout camps and tourist lodges. Having grown up on a small lake in Wisconsin, I know the smells and sounds of places like Spirit Lake: water dripping from a canoe paddle, the pounding of children's footsteps on boat docks, the kaboosh of their cannonballs in the lake, the shrilling of frogs on April nights, how the spring air startles with its sweetness as it fills a musty cabin that has been closed tight for the winter, the way words and laughter are snatched by the wind as neighbors converse on a lakeshore at night. The overlook suddenly feels strangely quiet.

On the way back to the car, I stop at a sign prohibiting off-trail wandering by visitors that was posted next to the remains of a charred tree lying prone and half buried in pumice. It reads: Reveg in Progress. Here and there, leafy clumps of low-growing plants emerge from earth that looks more like gravel than loamy, nurturing soil.

I suddenly realize that this is it—this is precisely what I came here to see: a ruffle of leaves in the sear, these frills of chlorophyll still pliable in the patter of November sleet. I hold a leaf in my fingers and close my eyes, half expecting that I might actually feel a pulse in this life that was audacious enough to put down roots in a place racked by the wind and shivered by cold.

The plant's persistence here is due, in part, to skills honed over evolutionary time. Like a Swiss army knife, every organism possesses an ingenious set of tools that are designed to meet multiple challenges. Adapting to change, however, requires more than a diverse portfolio of survival strategies. It's also about winning the luck of the draw in a game that sometimes might render such skills useless. The scientists who have studied the unfolding of life here in the aftermath of radical change point to a whole host of quixotic factors that determined what would prevail and what would succumb: the fact that the eruption occurred in the early morning rather than late afternoon or early spring rather than in the flush of summer, the fluctuations of rainfall in subsequent months or years; the fact that the volcano blew sideways to the north and largely spared its southern flanks.

Persistence, Mount St. Helens style, is about showing up, paying attention, adapting as best you can to the shifting world around you knowing all the while that life is an unspoken conspiracy of random forces, a risky and sometimes unnerving collaboration with chance that can sideswipe even the most attentive and skillful inhabitant.

•

Nearly every two weeks from 1981 to 1985, arachnologist Rod Crawford and his colleagues would leave Seattle and head south in the direction of Mount St. Helens. There was the obligatory stop for a burger at the Huff and Puff Drive-In in Randle. Then, he says, they would set out on the road to Windy Ridge, taking bets on whether or not "the outhouse at Windy Point had been blown over again," he recalls.

Two days before my trip to Mount St. Helens, I meet him in his office in the basement of the Thomas Burke Memorial Museum on the University of Washington campus in Seattle. We draw close around a lamp on a desk that is crammed with a computer and stacks of files. Behind us in the shadows are metal cabinets that store decades of taxonomic research. Crawford hardly needs to consult any of it since he easily retrieves information from the ready catalogue of his own memory.

He shows me a faded color photograph of himself in the early days of Mount St. Helens research. He is posing on the Pumice Plain, an expanse of drab rubble framed by the shell of the crater. If Crawford were wearing a space suit instead of T-shirt and khaki shorts, I would have guessed that he was standing on the moon.

It is here, on what looks like a far outpost of life, that Crawford and his University of Washington colleagues, among them the late John Edwards and his graduate student Patrick Sugg, pondered one of the most fundamental questions in ecology: What happens after all the living residents of a place have been extinguished, "cooked, buried, blown away or scoured clear," as they were on the Pumice Plain? In other words, What comes next after all is dispatched to hell in a handbasket?

Scientists use the classic theory of primary succession to help answer this question. The Mount St. Helens eruption would provide them with an ideal outdoor laboratory for testing its underlying assumptions. After all, "it's not every day that a volcano conveniently sterilizes 80 square kilometers of habitat," Crawford observes.

Primary succession posits that plants are responsible for triggering the reset button in bare mineral substrates such as sediments that had been newly exposed by scouring floods, a retreating glacier or, like the Toutle River Valley, buried and baked by a volcanic eruption. Among the first to take root are pioneer plants capable of tolerating the often-extreme conditions of a post-disturbance landscape—including intense solar radiation, drying winds or wide fluctuations in temperature. These hardy newcomers help build soil, for example, by trapping blowing particles of sediment or increase the availability of moisture and nutrients through their decaying remains. By ameliorating the raw conditions, they provide a toehold for other, more finicky plant species that gradually elbow them out of their habitat. Over time, even these intermediate plant communities are replaced by what is known as a climax community, i.e., a mature system with a relatively stable network of relationships that is able to persist until disturbance trips the cycle of succession all over again.

Mount St. Helens might easily have been cited as another textbook example of how plants initiate primary succession. In June 1982, a young ecologist named Charlie Crisafulli had been flying low to the ground in a helicopter, crisscrossing the Pumice Plain in search of any signs of life. "It was complete and utter barrenness," he recalls in a 2010 *Nova* documentary on Mount St. Helens. Suddenly, smack dab in the center of the Pumice Plain, Crisafulli spotted a splash of intense blue color sprouting from the gray rubble. It was a prairie lupine. He speculates that a seedpod had somehow been washed down from the higher elevations, where lupines customarily grow, and had taken root in the volcanic ash. These colorful, showy plants had a special advantage in the nutrient-poor conditions of the post-eruption landscape: they come equipped with their own fertilizer factory. Like other legumes, lupines host bacteria on their roots that can transform the abundant nitrogen in the air into a form that the plant can use. In exchange, the plant provides the bacteria with sugars from photosynthesis. Crisafulli promptly staked out a research plot around the lone volunteer and revisited the site year after year. Within a decade, this one individual lupine had spawned 169,000 descendants. Moreover, they helped to jumpstart the conditions that allowed numerous other plants and animals to colonize the plain and to build thriving communities of more diverse species. Lupines, for example, provided food for northern pocket gophers. In the process of tunneling their burrows, the animals kicked rich soils onto the mineral surface. These gopher mounds served as islands of hospitality that invited additional plants and animal to gain a toehold on the Pumice Plain.

The research by Edwards and his colleagues, however, would provide a surprising twist to this story by demonstrating that animals, not plants, were the triggers of primary succession on the Pumice Plain. During ground operations in the very first days after the eruption, search-and-rescue helicopter pilots reported seeing numerous insects on the Pumice Plain. These organisms could not have survived the massive disturbances on the Pumice Plain, nor could they have made the journey on foot since the nearest intact refugia was at least 11 miles away. Edwards and his colleagues reasoned that any arthropods that appeared on the plain in the early years had to have dropped out of the sky.

The appearance of what Edwards called the "parachute troops" wasn't altogether surprising. Scientists have long known that arthropods can travel far distances. Take spiders, for example. On Oct. 31, 1832, Charles Darwin aboard the *H.M.S Beagle* observed how spiders drifting on silk filaments, what he called "Aeronaut spiders," had accumulated on the ship's ropes. In his diary he remarked, "how inexplicable is the cause which induces these small insects...to undertake their aerial excursions," particularly since they were sailing at least 60 miles off the coast of Argentina, far beyond the possibility of landing in any suitable habitat.

Back in 1904, the author of a *New York Times* column entitled "Things Novel, Quaint and Curious" recounts a similar observation by George H. Dodge, an American steamship captain. In winter 1881-82 Dodge was piloting a vessel more than 200 miles off the eastern coast of South America when a wind from the direction of the continent blew a large squadron of eight-legged "Aeronauts" into the rigging.

Arachnologist Crawford points out that Darwin and Dodge were describing a behavior known as ballooning. A juvenile spider will climb to a high point—the top of a fence post or to the end of a tree limb, say—point its backside up into the air and then emit filaments of silk from spinneret organs located on the underside of its abdomen. The animal will adjust its position in the direction of the wind so that it can use its force to help unfurl the string. When enough silk is caught up in the breeze, the spider releases its hold and is carried aloft. Physicist Peter Gorham of the University of Hawaii recently published research suggesting that forces from the earth itself could give these threads an electrostatic charge that aids in keeping the spiderlings airborne and that they actually may seek out launch sites where charge densities are high.

On first glance, ballooning seems to be a hit-or-miss proposition. Many spiders will land in hostile terrain and die. Nonetheless, Crawford observes, there are advantages to undertaking the dicey journey. "Any organism that reproduces in considerable numbers has to disperse. If an orb weaver lays 900 eggs in one egg sac, the babies can't all live where mamma lived. They balloon to 'get away from it all,' " he says. Taking to the air in great numbers increases the odds that at least some spiderlings may find a home that allows them to survive and reproduce.

Crawford points out that there have been quite a few studies on the factors involved in take-off, but what happens after the arachnids become entrained in the wind is anyone's guess. "You can imagine the difficulties of such a study. You would have to find a spider that was about to balloon and attach some kind of telemetering device that wasn't too heavy to keep it from taking off," he says.

Crawford and his colleagues suspected, however, that the ecological impact of aerial spiders and other arthropods was significant. "On a summer's day," write Edwards and Sugg, "at least half the insect biomass may be airborne, a fact well known to swallows and swifts but little appreciated by earthbound humans."

Indeed, as early as 1926, researchers from the U.S. Bureau of Entomology and Plant Quarantine tried to identify and quantify the organisms in the earth's aerial plankton. Outfitting planes with special sticky traps, they began to fly sorties over Louisiana to learn more about the migrations of crop pests such as gypsy moths and cotton boll-worm moths. Their aerial reconnaissance, which lasted five years, yielded striking results. At any given time in the skies over one square mile of Louisiana countryside, at elevations ranging from 50 to 14,000 feet, the air column contained some 25 million to 36 million arthropods. Their catch included "ladybugs at 6,000 feet during the daytime, striped cucumber beetles at 3,000 feet during the night. They collected three scorpion flies at 5,000 feet, thirty-one fruit flies between 200 and 3,000, a fungus gnat at 7,000 and another at 10,000. They trapped anthrax-transmitting horsefly at 200 feet and another at 1,000. They caught wingless worker ants as high as 4,000 feet and sixteen species of parasitic ichneumon wasps at altitudes up to 5,000 feet. At 15,000 feet, 'probably the highest elevation at which any specimen has ever been taken above the surface of the earth,' they trapped a ballooning spider...." writes Hugh Raffles in his book *Insectopedia*.

These high-fliers do not circulate indefinitely, however. What then was the impact of all this winged biomass once it had dropped back down to earth? So few studies have examined this question largely because of one logistical difficulty:

it is impossible to distinguish resident biota on the ground from new arrivals that fall out of the sky. "The eruption of Mount St. Helens gave us the perfect opportunity to test the hypothesis that, microorganisms aside, arthropods [rather than plants] would be the true pioneers of the barren pyroclastic surfaces and the initiators of biological succession," Edwards and Sugg wrote.

As soon as the scientists got the green light from the USFS in 1981, they set about investigating their hunches by installing traps around Mount St. Helens. As points of comparison, they also sampled arthropods in the blowdown zone and on the south side of the mountain that was little impacted by the eruption. Their equipment was simple. At first, the researchers buried a series of plastic cups, setting their lips flush with the ground's surface. Each cup was partially filled with ethylene glycol that would trap and preserve the arthropods that wandered into them. When returning elk developed an unhealthy interest in slurping the cup's contents, Edwards designed another apparatus that was equally low-tech and effective—a wooden frame with fine screen on the bottom that trapped the aerial fallout while allowing rain to seep through. The frame was set into the ground and filled with golf balls to simulate the rough contours of the Pumice Plain's surface. "It turned out to be the magic data gatherer," Crawford says. The researchers visited the traps every two weeks during the field season for five years. On the Pumice Plain, they collected more than 100,000 arthropod specimens representing some 1,500 species. Insects made up nearly 80 percent of their catch, most of them flies and beetles. The remainder was largely made up of ballooning juvenile spiders.

Even the scientists were taken aback by quantity of arthropod fallout from the sky. "The surprising thing was the sheer magnitude of arrival that was going on," Crawford observes. "This had practically been unstudied before."

Most of the parachute troopers, however, were not adapted to survive the Pumice Plain's harsh conditions and quickly perished. Tephra abrades the waxy cuticles of arthropods, making them prone to lethal desiccation, a special hazard for organisms that have a high surface-to-volume ratio. Wide swings in temperature on the Pumice Plain, as well as inadequate cover from the sun and wind, were also problematic. Many could not find suitable food. Edwards called them the "derelicts of dispersal."

The doom of arthropod fallout, however, was not all gloom. Newly erupted volcanic sediments are so poor in essential nutrients, for example, that measurements of total organic carbon and nitrogen taken in 1980 near sampling sites on the Pumice Plain registered zero. Five years later, the amount of these nutrients in the pyroclastic-flow materials, while still low, had undergone a noticeable increase. The rain of material from the sky, a large fraction of which was composed of arthropods, was helping to gradually rebuild the fertile conditions for supporting new life. Moreover, it was doing so in subtle, almost covert, ways. Indeed, when the researchers examined the crevices of rubble on the Pumice Plain, they discovered small junkyards of arthropod remains, and wind-blown seeds germinating in what Edwards and Sugg called the "arthropod compost."

These derelicts of dispersal also provided food for the predators and scavengers that were able to survive and reproduce, the first of which were fellow airborne dispersers such as beetles and true bugs. The reliable rain of food allowed them to establish breeding populations on the Pumice Plain within three years of the eruption. By 1986, after a few isolated patches of vegetation had taken hold on the Pumice Plain, six species of spiders also had established breeding populations, some of which originated from a distance of 31 miles to the west.

The results of this research on Mount St. Helens led the researchers to conclude that the biomass that falls from the sky had been grossly underestimated and that arthropods can serve as the critical agents of primary succession in deeply disturbed landscapes. In the process, they rendered visible what was nearly invisible: diaphanous specks of life hitchhiking currents of air, parachuting to earth unbidden in a mysterious rain of particles that changed everything.

•

On my last day at the monument, I visit the Mount St. Helens Visitor Center. There in the gift shop I spot a cutout card with a colored drawing of Mount St. Helens in its heyday on the cover. It was a reference to the time not so long ago when the perfect symmetry of its lineaments earned it the nickname "Fujiyama of America": long fingers of snow draped over its crown like icing, a stippling of conifers on its lower flanks and, in the foreground, a section of the shoreline of Spirit Lake complete with a cluster of cabins and a sandy swimming beach. It looked like an ordinary day in July.

When I open the front flap of the card, however, I nearly gasp. There is a drawing of the post-eruption landscape, a Mr. Hyde lurking beneath the volcano's Dr. Jekyll: the menacing grin of Mount St. Helen's broken crater, its green slopes melted into a gray slurry, and Spirit Lake choked with ash and logs. It poses, through pictures, a simple question about the aftermath of catastrophic change: What now?

For nearly four decades, scientists have been answering this question on Mount St. Helens. The longevity of their patient, painstaking investigations is, in itself, an extraordinary achievement and an anomaly in the way science is typically conducted. In 1989, for example, the prestigious journal *Ecology* reported the results of a review of 749 papers that had been published over the prior decade. Only 1.7 percent of the total number of field studies was carried out over a period of at least five years. A similar study by biologist Patrick J. Weatherhead in 1986 reviewed 308 papers in major ecology, evolution and animal-behavior journals and found that the mean duration of these studies was 2.5 years, the average length of a research grant or the research phase of a graduate degree. These snapshots can skew the judgments we make about how nature really works. Mount St. Helens is a case in point. It took the eruption of a volcano in our midst and five years of diligent study to show us that there are oceans of animals in the air that can change the course of life on the ground.

Before the Stallion and I saddle up for what would be our final ride to Seattle, I take one last loop around a wetland on the center's grounds. The sun has burned off the mist around the peak of Mount St. Helens, and I finally get a glimpse of the snow-covered volcano, solitary, almost stand-offish, in the distance. Suddenly, I catch sight of an iridescent strand of silk floating in the air overhead, a flash of blue, then orange twisting this way and that like a live flame, then another strand and another. The air is filled with the fly lines of ballooning spiders. Had they tiptoed to the edge of some grass blades and patiently waited for a rare sunny day in a Pacific Northwest autumn to let loose their kite strings? Would they touch down in the reeds across the pond or become derelicts of dispersal in the rubble of the crater? Would some of the high-fliers make it to the Pacific coast, become entangled long enough in the riggings of a sailboat to cause the occupants to exclaim in won-der, as Darwin and others did before them?

Where would their collaboration with chance take them?

11

STRANGER DANGER: HOMELAND SECURITY IN THE FOREST

ABOUT 10 MILES SOUTH OF THE COLLEGE TOWN OF Missoula, Montana, is a remnant of the old West that is so rare you might be tempted to dismiss it as a figment of your imagination. "Every time I walk in here, I always stop and soak it in because it's so special," says Erick Greene, professor of wildlife biology at the University of Montana, Missoula.

Greene is referring to a centuries-old forest with magnificent stands of cottonwood, aspen and ponderosa pine that stretch a full 100 feet toward the sky. As if this weren't magical enough, running through it is the Bitterroot River, one of America's blue-ribbon trout streams. Somehow this patch was spared the fate of many riparian woodlands throughout the West in which river banks were logged to their edges and then converted to cattle pastures and alfalfa fields. Here, the Bitterroot was allowed to switchback across the land, carving oxbows that now form slackwater sloughs where harlequin-patterned wood ducks paddle. Moose, elk, mule deer, bear, mountain lions and wolves roam these forested reaches. Especially valuable to wildlife are the many snags. The dead standing trees serve as pantries, housing and nurseries for a wide range of wildlife, in particular, cavity-nesting birds. Greene and his students once sampled a random location in these snags and, within a 360-degree radius of where they stood, they counted about 60 nest cavities. "When I first came here," Greene recalls, "I was like, Oh my goodness. Look at all these dead trees. This is great. This is what riparian forests should be like, but you don't see many like this anymore."

For more than a decade, the forest has served as a laboratory for Greene's field work. But it's much more than that. Touring the site with him, as I did on a sunny morning last May, is like taking a stroll through a village in Italy with the resident mayor. He knows everyone's back story. At one point, Greene points to a bald-faced hornet and advises caution. In South America, he says, its painful sting has earned it the nickname *venti-quattro horas*, translated as "you'll be screaming for 24 hours." When asked if he's ever been stung, he answers with a nervous chuckle. Then Greene suddenly drops down on one knee to greet an old friend: *Phidippus*, a large jumping spider in the Salticidae family. "Look at that," he exclaims, admiring its saffron-colored back and abdomen. "That's a gorgeous spider. What a beauty." In 1987 he and his colleagues published a paper in the journal *Science* showing that the spider's prey—a tephritid fruit fly—had evolved an ingenious way to fend off a lethal attack. The fly's wings bear the lookalike pattern of the spider's legs. When stalked, the fly simply flicks its wings to imitate the territorial display of a spider rearing its legs. It's code for "You're trespassing. Back off or else." Although the spider possesses a bank of eight eyes, which Greene says gives it the best eyesight in the arthropod world, it is fooled by the fly's clever mimicry and instantly retreats. This work became a kind of scientific milestone, providing unusual documentation of an insect masquerading as its predator to avoid being eaten. Thanks to Greene's work, such biological ruses, once thought to be rare, are causing scientists to take another look at other similar cases.

•

These days, however, it's not the jousting between spiders and fruit flies that holds Greene's attention. For more than a decade, he has been studying homeland security—from a birds-eye perspective. As in his previous work, it relies on tuning in more closely to the ordinary world around him. And the scrutiny has produced results that are equally as groundbreaking.

Like humans, Greene points out, birds need to communicate danger, everything from the location and size of hazards to the urgency of the threats. His study site happens to be an ideal spot for eavesdropping on their intel. Although today's riparian forests occupy only an estimated one percent of semi-arid western landscapes, he says, 80-90 percent of birds use them at some point during their life cycle, be it feeding, breeding, migrating or resting. Their occupation of these forests is especially important in winter as birds descend from the snowy mountains to the lower-elevation valleys where they concentrate in protected places like Greene's study site. And that makes them especially attractive to a whole range of predators, from pygmy owls to sharp-shinned hawks, the fearsome F-22 fighter jets of the avian world.

So how do they evade the talons of hungry raptors? By listening in on each other's conversation, Greene says. He notes that alarm calls and behaviors can sometimes be so subtle that even woods-wise birders and naturalists can miss them. Through sophisticated and painstaking analyses of spectrograms (graphical representations of sound), however, he has been able to interpret the communication of forest inhabitants. Study results demonstrate how nuanced and effective such forest chatter can be at protecting them from predators.

It takes a village to do this work. Greene recruits a small volunteer army of student workers who will swarm the study site on a calm winter day. The team mounts a collection of 16 synchronized microphones at various heights on the trees, which he says is among the largest arrays ever erected for these kinds of behavioral experiments. When all is in place, Greene hits the record button to capture several minutes of ordinary forest sounds. Then he will issue a trigger that he says is designed to "piss the birds off." For approximately two minutes, he will play several types of sounds: the call of a raptor, the alarm calls of different species of birds or a raucous audio recording of enraged songbirds mobbing an enemy such as a northern pygmy owl, a four-inch-tall owl with a voracious appetite for their kind. The faux distress calls will draw a wide range of curious birds—including black-capped chickadees, mountain chickadees, chestnut-backed chickadees, red-breasted nuthatches, white-breasted nuthatches, woodpeckers and Steller's jays. Soon the live birds will join the fray with their own alarms. For the next five minutes, he will record their frenzied responses. In recent years, he has created even more ingenious triggers—roboraptors. Enlisting the services of a taxidermist as well as those of a talented undergraduate physics student, Greene has created mechanized replicas of seven different species of hawks and owls. It includes a pygmy owl cyborg of feathers, motors and computer boards that even swivels its head like the real thing. The impersonators are hidden inside fake stumps that fall away at the touch of a button on a modified garage-door opener. The decoys are so convincing that they never fail to attract an angry horde of birds. Curiously, the smaller birds such as chickadees and nuthatches accost the pint-sized owl with greater vehemence than many of the larger predators, perhaps because small forest birds make up some 90 percent of the pygmy owl's diet.

Each experiment may last only eight minutes, but it requires months of data crunching in the lab. Subsequent analysis of these field recordings — what Greene calls "decoding the info-scape" —has produced astounding insights. For starters, Greene has discovered that the language that birds use to communicate threat is highly specialized. To alert forest dwellers to the presence of a perched raptor in the neighborhood, for example, birds will use what Greene refers to as a "mobbing call." These harsh, easily pinpointed signals utilize a wide bandwidth that can penetrate far into the forest. They are a flash mob alert for every bird within earshot. Indeed, studies have documented that such calls are capable of luring a whopping 50 different species of birds to a mobbing event. It seems counterintuitive to draw birds to danger, Greene says, but perched raptors, since they are not flying and actively hunting, pose less threat to their smaller, far more maneuverable prey. The defensive recruits position themselves on branches around the stationary hawk or owl, forming a kind of halo of scolding, shrieking and dive-bombing birds. Their message to the raptor is clear, Greene says: "You're busted. Time to get out of Dodge."

By contrast, birds use a far different language to communicate the sighting of a raptor that is actively hunting in flight. Their Code Red alert, which signals the most extreme danger, has a dramatically different acoustical signature from the mobbing call. At 6 to 10 kilohertz, the call falls outside the sound-frequency interval that raptors are good at hearing. This short, thin, higher-frequency sound is known as a "seet" call. Birds instantly respond by either diving for cover or freezing in place. Most astounding, however, is his discovery that these high-alert calls are like batons passed along bird by bird in a sonic relay race. So speedy is this broadcasting system that Greene has clocked seet calls traveling through the forest at speeds of 100 mph, far exceeding the capacity of even the fastest forest flyers to keep up, including the top gun Sharp-shinned hawk, which approaches velocities of 60 mph.

When birds speak, the forest listens. So important is this language, that even unrelated species have adopted some of its vocabulary. Greene notes that red squirrels and chipmunks, which also are vulnerable to attack from the skies, also give mobbing and seet calls similar to their avian neighbors, even though the anatomy of their voice structures couldn't be more different. "Squirrels understand 'bird-ease,' and birds understand 'squirrel-ease,' " he quipped in a 2015 New York Times article.

Given that forest animals collectively mount such a successful defense, how do raptors ever score a meal? It's a question that fills Greene with admiration for birds like hawks. "It's really hard to be a hawk," he observed in a 2016 interview on the Cornell Lab of Ornithology website. "You're hunting and flying around, trying to find your dinner, and yet there's this bow wave of information out in front of you faster than you can ever fly."

Greene cites anecdotal evidence suggesting that "a lot of the hunting strategies of raptors are designed to try to subvert this early warning system," he observes. A common ruse, according to a falconer he knows who flies a pair of Cooper's hawks for hunting, is for one of the pair to provoke a mobbing event by flying and perching in a conspicuous way. While the attention of the agitated birds is diverted, the mate will sidle onto a nearby branch and then dive in for a kill.

Other raptors have honed stealth and surprise to a fine art, especially around backyard feeders. Greene has watched hawks take advantage of cryptic coloration by positioning themselves up against tree trunks at dawn to quietly await the early arrivals at feeders. Others have perfected an aerial artistry that leaves even veteran scientists like Greene wide-eyed and slack-jawed with wonder. "I once watched a Sharp-shin fly Mach 2, just scream down the alley behind my house, flying underneath parked cars and around garbage cans, doing everything he could to stay under the radar," he recalls. The hawk concluded these maneuvers by seamlessly vaulting an eight-foot-tall hedge to mount a surprise attack at a feeder on the other side.

Greene could be conducting any number of controlled experiments from the warmth and comfort of a university office, but these kinds of episodic encounters are central to his scientific inquiries, even if it means regularly venturing into the freezing temperatures of a Montana winter. "It's more difficult, and it's messier," he observed in the *New York Times*. "But it's glorious nature."

ADELHEID FISCHER IS CO-DIRECTOR OF InnovationSpace, a sustainable product-development program at Arizona State University. She leads the program's biomimicry initiative, which introduces students to the use of biology as a means of sustainable innovation in design, business and engineering. She also serves as assistant director of ASU's Biomimicry Center.

Fischer is a writer who focuses on natural history, ecology and environmental history. She has written for many publications, including *Utne Reader*, *Orion*, *Conservation*, *Places* and *Arizona Highways*. She is co-author of *Valley of Grass: Tallgrass Prairie and Parkland of the Red River Region*, winner of a Minnesota Book Award for Nature Writing, and *North Shore: A Natural History of Minnesota's Superior Coast*. In 2014 she received the Ellen Meloy Desert Writers Award. She is working on a book that explores the ecology of grief and loss in the sky islands of southeastern Arizona.

Fischer makes her home at the foot of South Mountain in Phoenix, Arizona, where she shares her yard, and sometimes her house, with nighthawks, southern house spiders, scorpions, coyotes, cactus wrens, and the occasional javelina.

•